HOME IS WHERE THE OFFICE IS

Andrew Bibby # HOME IS WHERE THE OFFICE IS

•

A PRACTICAL
HANDBOOK
FOR
TELEWORKING
FROM HOME

•

British Library Cataloguing in Publication Data

Bibby, Andrew
 Home is where the office is.
 I. Title
 658.02

ISBN 0 340 55951 9

First published 1991

© 1991 Andrew Bibby

All rights reserved. No part of this publication may be reproduced or transmitted in any form or by any means, electronic or mechanical, including photocopy, recording, or any information storage and retrieval system, without permission in writing from the publisher or under licence from the Copyright Licensing Agency Limited. Further details of such licences (for reprographic reproduction) may be obtained from the Copyright Licensing Agency Limited, of 90 Tottenham Court Road, London, W1P 9HE.

Typeset by Multiplex Techniques Ltd, Orpington
Printed in Great Britain for the educational publishing division of Hodder & Stoughton Ltd, Mill Road, Dunton Green, Sevenoaks, Kent by Richard Clay Ltd, St. Ives plc, Bungay, Suffolk.

CONTENTS

1	Introduction	5
2	Teleworking: the idea	11
3	Making the decision: is telework right for you?	20
	Career questions	21
	Self-discipline and work motivation	24
	Space	25
	Location: where to telework	26
	Children, childcare	30
	Family relationships	32
	Financial and employment implications	34
	Longer-term implications	37
	Further information	39
4	Telework and the telephone	40
	Telephone service providers	45
	LinkLines	46
	Answering facilities and paging	47
	Services from digital exchanges	48
	Videoconferencing	49
	Mobile communications	49
	Fax	51
5	Going on-line: an introduction to computer communications	54
	Microcomputers and modems	55
	Modem speeds	57
	Data bits and Parity checking	59

Comms software	59
Making the most of on-line time	61
Packet switching	62
An example: accessing Telecom Gold	63
Further reading	65

6 What's available on-line?: 1   Information databases   67

Example: Phone Base	69
Example: Electronic Yellow Pages (EYP)	70
Example: Profile	71
Example: ICC UK companies database	73
Example: ABI/Inform	74
Database hosts	74
Other on-line hosts	77
Help and information	78

7 What's available on-line?: 2   Videotex   80

An introduction to Prestel	81
Government information	83
BT on-line directories	84
Travel	84
Home banking and shopping	84
Communications	85
Prestel charges and access arrangements	85
Télétel	86

8 What's available on-line?: 3   Communications   87

Direct computer-to-computer links	87
Electronic mail	88
Bulletin boards	91
On-line conferences	92
CompuServe	94

9 The technicalities of telework — 96

- Planning issues — 96
- Mortgage lenders and landlords — 97
- Insurance — 98
- Business rates and local taxation — 98
- Taxation and business expenditure — 100
- Self-employed or employed? — 102
- Health and Safety at Work Act — 103
- Data Protection Act — 104

10 Help when it's needed — 106

- OwnBase — 106
- Telecommuting Powerhouse — 107
- ACRE — 107
- *Live Wire* — 108
- Health and safety advice — 108
- Telecottages: out from the home — 111

Appendix 1: Packet switching using BT's Dialplus service — 113

Appendix 2: Further reading — 116

Index — 119

ACKNOWLEDGEMENTS

Many people have helped me in the work of preparing this book – to them my thanks. In particular, I acknowledge the assistance offered by the staff of the library at the Manchester Business School and the library of the University of Manchester Institute of Science and Technology.

An especial acknowledgement is necessary to record the help and encouragement provided by Jane Scullion.

1
INTRODUCTION

The idea is a seductive one. Outside your window, the wind is scudding the clouds across the moors, tugging at the heather and the cotton-grass. A handful of hardy sheep are chomping away peacefully beside an old stone wall. There's a buzzard high up in the sky, and from across the other side of the valley the sound of a curlew calling.

Inside, however, it's just another ordinary working day. You're at home, at your desk, at work. In a corner of the room a fax machine is stuttering out a message from an office somewhere down in London's docklands – you'll look at it later.

Your personal computer meanwhile is hooked up to the telephone line and communicating with a mainframe computer in California. The information you need for your work is spilling out on to the colour monitor, at the cost of $5 a minute. But the cost doesn't matter: in ten minutes you'll have all the facts you'll need over the next fortnight saved safely to the hard disk.

This is the future of work.

Or at least, this could be the future of work for some of us. It's called 'teleworking' or 'telecommuting', and the idea is that instead of travelling in to work each day we wait at home for the work to be delivered to us, courtesy of the latest in information technology.

No longer will we need to live within daily commuting distance of our workplace. No longer will we have to suffer the strain and time-wasting involved in riding the rush hour. And no longer will we have to separate our work life from our family and home life – if we want to break off from writing a report or checking the figures on a spreadsheet to play with the children or take the dog for a walk, well why shouldn't we?

Teleworkers can turn their back on city life, and chase the dream of living in the country. If you decide that you want to live in a converted shepherd's cottage half way up a mountain track, that shouldn't be a problem. Exmoor, the Pennines or the Scottish Highlands are as well-placed for teleworking as a flat in central London.

There are other possibilities: equip yourself with a mobile telephone and a stack of batteries, and you could convert a caravan into a travelling office and home, and head for the open road. Or perhaps you might prefer to make your base in a narrow boat, floating peacefully through the canal network of central England.

What's more, telework is not confined by national boundaries. So the shepherd's cottage need not necessarily be in Britain: you might prefer instead to set up your workbase in a farmhouse in the Auvergne or an old Tuscan hill-top fort. It could even be feasible to telework from a yacht permanently cruising the Greek islands or the West Indies (though the satellite telecommunications bills might be a little steep).

Two hundred years back, the first industrial revolution drove people away from the rural areas into the newly expanding cities, and away from home-based work into the factories. The suggestion that another technological revolution now gives us the opportunity of reversing this process is an intriguing one. But can it really be true? Is the wheel of history really turning full circle?

Some people are certainly making big claims about teleworking. Business consultants employed to research the possibilities of this form of working for the Confederation of British Industry and British Telecom (who not surprisingly are pretty excited at the implications for their profits) claimed in 1988 that 7,044,000 full-time employees were already doing jobs which could potentially be undertaken, at least partially, from home. The figure swelled by a further three million if allowance were made for part-timers and self-employed people.

In fact, the organisation which conducted the research, the Henley Centre for Forecasting, concluded that by 1995 49.7% of all employees – or about 14 million people in all – could in theory be teleworking.

These statistics don't include, of course, some types of work: assembly line workers in car factories won't find it very easy to perform their work from home, for example. But there are numerous other jobs where, it is suggested, teleworking is a possibility: professionals of various kinds, clerical workers, sales people, supervisory staff, administrators. What these people all have in common is one thing – their work depends, at least in part, on processing or using information.

The point is this: as long as the information you need to use for your work is held, say, in a filing cabinet, it's obviously sensible to have your office conveniently located nearby. But if that information is held on a computer, there is no longer the same necessity for your workplace to be geographically close: the details you need can be extracted from the computer, through dedicated data lines or just through the ordinary telephone lines, regardless of whether the computer database is located in the next room, in a building the other side of town, in another town or even in another country. Provided you have a power supply and access in some way to the telephone network you are free to undertake your work where you choose.

The Henley Centre for Forecasting researchers were quick to point out that their report didn't necessarily mean that many millions of British people *would* soon find themselves working from home: there were all sorts of physical and psychological reasons, they stressed, which could encourage people to continue commuting in to a central workplace. Furthermore, as the report made clear, the 49.7% total included people who would only be able to undertake part of their total overall work load by teleworking from a remote location. Nevertheless, the central message of the report was clear: teleworking is an idea which could have fundamental implications for our society.

Even quite a small growth in the number of people working from home could have some intriguing consequences, it pointed out. Since teleworkers will be able to dress as they please for their work 'there will be less demand for formal clothing and greater demand for casual clothing'. There will be fewer people in the cities: 'Pubs, cafes, sandwich bars and restaurants catering to the business community at lunchtimes and after work will suffer' (though fortunately 'there will, however, be compensating opportunities in residential areas...').

Newsagents at stations will lose trade, and there will be less commuting time available for reading: 'Books, newspapers and magazines will all feel the effects.'.

The property market may also be affected, as workers gradually migrate away from London and the South-East to the Midlands, the South-West or further afield.

More seriously, the report points out that there are likely to be fewer road accidents if less people have to commute to work. A 20% drop in the number of miles driven to work could not only save lives but, also, it suggests, save the country as much as £93m.

Others have also spent time considering the implications of a teleworking society. Two American writers Marcia M Kelly and Gil E Gordon, for example, enjoyed a romp through some of the more far-fetched side-effects of teleworking at the end of a rather more sober analysis of the subject. Dentists and dieting organisations could be on to a winner, they maintained: 'Demand for both will grow for telecommuters who can't keep their snacking under control.'. Indeed, to save their staff from the dangers of excess gorging, employers might have to step in and purchase 'remote-controlled refrigerator locks for telecommuters' homes'.

Kitchen manufacturers would have to adjust, too. Kelly and Gordon predicted a new market for larger sinks 'to handle dishes piled up through the day by telecommuters'. But there could be potential bad news for pharmaceutical companies: 'The market for cold and flu remedies drops off as fewer people get sick from being close to ill co-workers.'.

And quail farmers would face a particularly grim future. Quail farmers? Ah, but of course: 'Quail farms may suffer because fewer executives are around to frequent classy restaurants for gourmet lunches.'.

The telework concept, in other words, can get the gastric juices of the imagination flowing freely. But the ideas can sometimes run ahead of the reality. Sometimes it seems as though everybody is talking about teleworking – and nobody is doing it. For example, according to one report, an international conference in Bonn in 1987 on the subject attracted 120 delegates from fourteen countries – only four of whom had ever been home-based workers: 'The rest were academics, researchers, theorists, sociologists, psychologists, consultants, bandwagon manipulators and ergonometricians.'.

Indeed a careful look at the available statistics by one British researcher, Mike Brocklehurst, recently concluded that the number of people in this country who were actually teleworking was no more than 80,000, 'and was probably substantially less'.

This book is intended to reflect the reality of telework, rather than the rhetoric. It's a practical handbook, designed to be of use for people who are actually teleworking, or are seriously considering working from home using new technology. I examine the disadvantages as well as the advantages, and don't assume that everyone should rush to set up a high-tech workstation in a corner of their living room. I also attempt to cover the sort of day-to-day concerns which home-based teleworkers are likely to face: from how to cope with childcare to how to make a computer modem work properly.

It is a book which has emerged from my own experience of teleworking from home, first from a house in the centre of a west Midlands city (where a hundred years before a master watchmaker had himself worked from home – the house still had the large windows of his first floor workshop) but now from a small town in West Yorkshire.

It is perhaps an appropriate place to be living when writing about new technology and home-based work. Up on the hills are the cottages where for many generations families combined hand-loom weaving with subsistence farming, before the Industrial Revolution transformed the area. The mills in the valleys sucked in men, women and children who previously had earned their livelihood by their own efforts at home: humiliation for proud people who had once been able to set their own hours of work, even to the extent of taking an extra day's break from work at the weekend to celebrate the feast of 'Saint Monday'.

Many of the mills are now closed, others are tourist attractions, while there are computer screens gleaming behind the mullions of at least some of the old weavers' houses. It seems significant that a few feet away, as I write, the towpath of the old canal which helped to bring industrialisation to this valley is being excavated to lay new optical fibre cables for Mercury Communications's digital network.

Technological change brings dangers (the Luddites, who roamed the hills a few miles south of here, knew all about the dangers) and opportunities. Telework is one of the changes which may be coming.

2
TELEWORKING: THE IDEA

'We're here to celebrate the birth of a new breed of worker,' Iain Vallance, the Chairman of British Telecom, announced grandly. 'He is the teleworker, or telecommuter – the person who travels to work, not down the Piccadilly line but down the telephone line, and who arrives at the office without actually leaving home.'

Mr Vallance was setting the scene at the start of a conference which BT had called jointly with the Confederation of British Industry (CBI), and which was held in September 1988 at London's Queen Elizabeth II centre a stone's throw from Westminster Abbey. Its title was 'Tomorrow's Workplace' – and tomorrow's workplace, it was implied, might turn out not to be the factory or city office block but instead simply: the home.

The speakers were a mixed, but generally prestigious, bunch. John Banham, the director general of the Confederation of British Industry (CBI), was there, as was Sir John Harvey-Jones the former ICI chairman. Also present was Norman Willis, general secretary of the Trades Union Congress.

Some conference participants seized on the opportunities that teleworking could provide for improving individual workers' quality of life. 'We are at the start of the third great transport revolution,' enthused Andrew Neil, the editor of the Sunday Times. He made the point that geographical distances had been overcome by technology, and predicted: 'A lot of your children and certainly your grand-children will be able to live on the beach in Malibu, or on the ski slopes of Colorado, or in the mountains of Scotland or wherever they would like to live and telecommute daily via their computers.'.

Others were more concerned with the benefits which teleworking could bring to business. These benefits included the possibility of lower salary levels (no need for expensive London pay supplements or for employers to compensate for high commuting expenses, perhaps), reduced equipment costs (if teleworkers paid some of these costs themselves), and higher productivity. Teleworkers could be as much as four times more productive than their equivalent office-based colleagues, it was claimed.

There were also significant savings which could be made in office overheads. This was a point taken up by another speaker, Bridget Blow of the FI Group, a company which has pioneered the use of home-based workers. Traditional work patterns, based around centrally-situated and expensive office blocks, might not be the most cost-effective way of organising work, she argued. 'To achieve 100% use of the capital tied up in an office block, it needs to be used 365 days a year. Usage reduces to 24% when time is taken out for holidays and the conventional five day, eight hour working week. This is before sick leave, lateness, early leaving, lunch breaks and social activity take their toll.' Take all this into account, and the real use of the building could be as low as 2% or 3%, she maintained. 'Think about that when you are paying £50 per square foot to keep your rubbish bin in your office in London!,' she added.

In other words, teleworking may be good news both for the individual (bye-bye Mitcham, hello Malibu) and for business. As *The Times* reported the next day, the senior industrialists present were able to go away at the day's end with the vision of a working revolution which could 'turn the country into a happier and safer place in which to live'.

The BT/CBI conference was not the first attempt there has been to ponder the changes which teleworking could bring. The classic prediction of a future spent in electronic home-working had been made almost ten years earlier in 1980 by Alvin Toffler, in his book *The Third Wave*.

Toffler, who has made something of a specialism of turning futurological forecasting into a popular science (his earlier book, *Future Shock*, was like *The Third Wave* a publishing bestseller) describes vividly one possible future lifestyle, taking his readers on a guided tour down a teleworking street: 'We would find many homes... in which man and wife split a single full-time job,' he writes. 'For example, we might find both husband and wife taking turns at monitoring a complex manufacturing process on the console screen in the den, four hours on, four hours off... Right next door (continuing our survey) we could well come upon a couple holding two different jobs but sharing *both*, the husband working as a part-time insurance planner and part-time as an architect's assistant, with the wife doing the same work on alternating shifts...' Children, too, Toffler avers, could be reintegrated into the world of work, and play their part in the family's telework life. 'In short, the spread of work-at-home on a large scale could not only affect family structure but transform relationships within the family,' he concludes.

Toffler came up with the phrase 'the electronic cottage' to describe his idea of the telework base of the future. It is a well-chosen and powerfully evocative term, suggestive both of high-tech glamour and old-world rural charm. (Somehow a future spent working in an 'electronic house' or 'electronic flat' seems considerably less attractive.)

But though Toffler's book popularised the idea, he was not the first to foresee a future spent teleworking from home. In the early Seventies, at the time of the oil crisis when the USA and Western Europe were anxiously counting the cost for their economies of increased energy prices, a Californian academic Jack Nilles put forward the idea of substituing 'telecommuting' for traditional commuting to work. Nilles was one of the first to point out that advances in computing and telecommunications were making it possible for much traditional office-based work to be undertaken from remote locations, including from the home.

Perhaps appropriately enough, therefore, the telework idea can be traced back to Californian roots, the state associated variously with new technology (Silicon Valley), with new age thinking, and (in Los Angeles at least) with some of the worst traffic problems for commuters in the world.

But it has also been California that has produced a powerful reminder that teleworking has its snags, too. In 1982 a local insurance firm, California Western States Life Insurance Company, offered some of its claims staff the chance to work from their homes instead of from the office. Most of the workers affected were women, and most were enthusiastic about the idea – at least to start with. But the problem was that the company had arranged for its teleworkers to be independent contractors, paid only on a piece-work basis and no longer eligible for the normal employees' benefits.

Gradually, the implications of this change became all too obvious. At the end of 1985, eight of the women gave up their jobs and immediately began to sue their former employer, claiming that the independent contracting arrangement was merely a subterfuge to enable the firm to avoid its employment responsibilities. Together the women's claim was for back benefits of $250,000, together with $1m added on for punitive damages.

The story ended three years later. A short news item in an American business magazine in October 1988 reported simply: 'Last January the company dropped its telecommuting programme and in May the employees settled out of court for an undisclosed sum.'

It is well to be a little cautious therefore before assuming that teleworking will automatically mean that everyone lives happily ever after. For some the chance to work at home can be a welcome perk, an opportunity to escape from the daily commuting grind and the necessity of living in a city suburb; there may be the advantages to be relished of having more time to spend with the family or indulging in new leisure interests. But for other people, teleworking can mean isolation and exploitation.

There is nothing new about home-based workers, especially women homeworkers, encountering low pay and poor working conditions. As the researcher Mike Brocklehurst has pointed out, 'It is important to realise that homeworking and new technology are not new bedfellows; there are historical precedents. In their time, the sewing machine, the typewriter and the knitting machine were new technologies that very quickly became used in the home. Yet homeworkers who use such equipment are often found amongst the very lowly paid. Will homeworkers who use computers be any different?'.

As early as 1982, the Equal Opportunities Commission had decided to try to find out. A study, carried out for the EOC by researcher Ursula Huws and later published as *The New Homeworkers*, investigated the experiences of seventy-eight teleworkers, almost all women, the majority of whom were computer professionals in their thirties. The study discovered that, while many of the workers appreciated the flexibility of home-based work, their average pay levels were significantly lower than similarly qualified office-based workers could expect to earn; the teleworkers who were self-employed also fared less well than those who were employees, facing both lower levels of earnings and fewer work benefits.

This distinction, between those people who are self-employed teleworkers and those who remain as employees, is important and one we shall consider again in this book. Strictly speaking, it may be correct to say that Jack Nilles's term 'telecommuting' and the equivalent British term 'teleworking' referred originally just to the working arrangement where a member of staff continued to work for an employer, albeit not from the employer's premises. However, this usage seems unhelpfuly restrictive, particularly given the changes in economic organisation over the past ten years and the growth of self-employment. I prefer a wider definition. (As will already have become clear, I also favour in this book the more usual British term 'teleworking' rather than the north American alternative, 'telecommuting', though the two terms are essentially synonymous. I also take a fairly relaxed attitude to the academic debate about what particular technological work tools are necessary before an activity can be labelled as telework: I am happy to proceed on the basis that telework may encompass many different work activities and occupations, different forms of work organisation, and indeed work locations. What teleworkers have in common is that they are making use of new computer and telecomms technology to practice some form of remote working.)

The evidence to date suggests that the number of employers who embrace the idea of allowing their employees to telework from home may be relatively small, and that in many more cases teleworkers are likely to find themselves working as self-employed contractors. For many people, self-employment may be itself a liberating experience, as liberating perhaps as the opportunity of working from home. But as the women workers at the California Western States Life Insurance company discovered, it can also represent a move away from established employment rights. In other words, there is a danger, especially perhaps for clerical workers engaged in more mechanical work, that the positive connotations of 'home' may be being used to try to get people to accept poorer employment conditions.

Indeed, some observers have suggested that telework is merely another aspect of a move by companies towards distinguishing between their 'core' and their 'peripheral' areas of business. It makes strong economic sense, it is argued, for a large firm to sub-contract much of its work to smaller peripheral companies (or indeed to individual contractors), who can be made to take many of the risks inherent in a fluctuating economic environment. In other words a dual economy may be developing, where a small number of powerful slimmed-down companies can preserve their performance records and profitability by making use of the clusters of smaller sub-contractors which surround them; in times of expansion more work is passed out to the peripheral firms, but when recession strikes it is this sub-contract work which can be cut back.

In the same way, some people argue, firms can find it profitable to make a distinction between their 'core' and 'peripheral' staff. 'When profits are threatened or reductions in expenditure necessary, management distinguishes between those workers who are essential to the long-term profitability of the organisation (core workers) and those who are disposable (peripheral workers)', wrote Sean Connolly in an industrial management journal in 1988. And the authors of a more recent study, *Telework: Towards the Elusive Office*, warn that, 'the greater freedom from central control experienced by some professional-level teleworkers may be based on an illusion resulting from an alteration in the mechanism used to exercise managerial control. Direct means of control have been replaced by indirect ones.'.

Arguably, there is already evidence of just such a process taking place in Britain. Rank Xerox were one of the first British companies to explore the teleworking idea, when in the early 1980s they faced the task of reducing their overhead costs in their London office. Rank Xerox encouraged selected volunteers to leave their employment and to found their own businesses, trading at arm's length with the parent firm. The first of these teleworking 'networkers', as Rank Xerox called them, started out in 1981, and by 1985 the number had grown to over fifty.

Rank Xerox offered an initial contract for services with each 'networker', but insisted that this work constituted no more than 50% of the teleworker's total income. The firm also made it a condition that each 'networker' established their own limited company (a legal structure which could have been inappropriate for some of the individuals involved, but which had the advantage of protecting the parent firm from potential Inland Revenue accusations that the 'networkers' were still effectively employees).

A generally upbeat account of the 'networking' experiment (written in 1985 in conjunction with Rank Xerox) suggested that in many cases teleworkers were happy with their experiences. But even those who were developing successful small businesses commented on the change in their legal situation. 'You quickly realise how vulnerable you are compared to your old situation, and the protection offered to you through what are regarded as standard terms of employment for large companies. It suddenly becomes obvious how valuable pensions, insurance, sick pay, holiday pay and BUPA are!', wrote the first networker, Roger Walker.

Another early proponent of home-based work has been the computer software consultancy company FI Group (formerly F International, where the 'F' originally stood for 'freelance'). The FI Group was established in 1962 and has been built up predominantly using freelance 'panel members', operating from home on a self-employed basis. The company has a core of employees, but about three-quarters of its regular workers are self-employed. The FI Group is sometimes described as the first teleworking company (though it was slow to make use of computer communications and information technology in its internal organisation).

However it would be wrong to give the impression that all the British experiments with teleworking to date have been on the basis of using self-employed contractors. Another much-quoted example is that of ICL, which has had two divisions predominantly staffed by home-based teleworking employees. Over the past few years, too, a number of local authorities have been developing schemes to allow selected employees to telework from their homes.

Telework, though, is not just a British phenomenon. Indeed, potentially at least, teleworking crosses national boundaries. It is technically almost as easy to work down the telephone line for an employer or client in Brussels, New York or Tokyo as for one in London. Conversely, as Andrew Neil's remark points out, there is no technical reason why a British person could not choose to telework from a home-base somewhere in the sun abroad, using the international telephone networks to send and receive data to and from Britain.

Teleworking opens up the possibility of the internationalisation of work, therefore. Already, in fact, some North American employers are sub-contracting basic data-entry or word processing work to overseas locations. Several US based companies already make use of agencies set up in Caribbean islands, particularly in Barbados. Another US firm has arranged for the data entry work for its magazine subscription database to be undertaken in the Irish Republic.

In each case, the impetus is the same: to transfer low-grade clerical work to parts of the world where labour costs are cheaper. 'We can do the work in Barbados for less than it costs in New York to pay for the floor space,' the company chairman of a US data entry company was reported to have said. Here perhaps is another example, this time a geographical one, of the development of the idea of a 'core' and a 'periphery' in business operation – and another warning, perhaps, that teleworking can raise some awkward issues.

To sum up, therefore: there is no doubt that teleworking offers the promise of change. The idea is intriguing and attractive. Plug in a computer to the telephone line and a world awaits. Why stay put in the suburbs when you could be out in the country, overlooking the hills or the sea? Why spend wasted time commuting when you could stroll a few yards downstairs each morning, and immediately reach your workplace? Why travel to your work when your work could come to you?

The electronic cottage in the country seems to offer an answer to a million city-dwellers' fantasies. And it seems to offer the promise of a more integrated lifestyle – combining the pleasures of work with the satisfaction of more time with family and friends.

But, as this chapter has tried to examine, there is a downside to teleworking as well. For some people, the advantages will outweigh the disadvantages. For others, the dream could turn quickly to a nightmare. The next chapter looks, in more practical detail, at the sort of issues to be considered before deciding whether or not to take the plunge.

3
MAKING THE DECISION: IS TELEWORK RIGHT FOR YOU?

Enjoying your weekends and holidays at home – even having the odd day working at home, perhaps to catch up with reading or to polish off a report – is one thing. Working full-time at home is a different experience. Will it work out?

It can be tempting to act on impulse, and sometimes decisions taken in this way turn out to be the right ones. But careful thought and some detailed planning in advance, weighing up the pros and cons, is likely to be better in the long run.

Business advisers recommend that anyone considering going into business draws up a formal 'business plan' before getting started. Only after you've undertaken the background market research and worked out the financial projections, they say, will you know if the business opportunity which has caught your eye is really such a good idea – and whether you are temperamentally suited to the work.

Similarly, background research and some careful costings may be appropriate for anyone contemplating a life as a teleworker, before the decision is taken. Despite the implication in the term 'telecommuting', the opportunity to save on the daily expense and effort of commuting to work is probably likely to turn out eventually to be quite a minor consideration.

This chapter examines one by one a number of different areas where a decision to telework from home may have implications for you. These are:

- career questions
- self-discipline and work motivation
- space
- location: where to telework
- children, childcare
- family relationships

- financial and employment implications
- longer-term implications

It may be that parts of this chapter seem to give a gloomy assessment of the teleworking experience. That's not my intention – although it is necessary to counter the very uncritical approach to telework which some people have encouraged. It's also better to be fully aware of any possible future snags and problems before you take the decision.

In any case, everybody's work and home situation is different. Some of these concerns will not apply to you, and you may have others to add to your own list.

Not everyone will have the luxury of being able to weigh up the pros and cons so dispassionately. For some people, changing over to teleworking may be the only practical way of avoiding giving up working for a particular employer: this could be the situation facing you, for example, if your partner or spouse is being asked to relocate or wants to move to a new job in a different part of the country.

Other people with domestic or family responsibilities may feel that home-based work is the only type of paid work that they are currently able or prepared to undertake.

For others, again, disabilities may limit their opportunity to obtain employment away from the home (though there can be dangers for able-bodied people in assuming that teleworking is automatically an appropriate work option for disabled people).

But whatever your particular circumstances, it makes sense to anticipate some of the issues which you are likely to face as a teleworker. Teleworking is not, ultimately, a technological issue but a human one.

Career questions

'Suicidal': that was the word used by one American woman to describe the effect that even part-time working from home would have on her career.

In orthodox career terms, it is probably a rash move to remove yourself from the office environment. You may be undertaking exactly the same work from home as you did before at your office desk, you may indeed be working more efficiently and improving your productivity, but unfortunately the maxim does seem true: if you are out of sight, you may be out of mind.

Telework is, as we have seen, an attractive theme for the one-off day conference in London; it has also become by now the subject of a considerable body of writing in personnel and management journals. But the reality is that, as yet, very few companies have much practical experience of teleworking. Suggesting to your boss or personnel manager, therefore, that you are interested in working from home is still likely to be viewed as an eccentric request. It is certainly not the most obvious way for you to be marked out as ambitious for greater responsibility and promotion.

Given that most methods of management still rely on monitoring whether an employee is physically present and working (or at least giving the impression of working) – rather than assessing job performance in terms, say, of the quality of the work produced – homeworkers will obviously be disadvantaged in terms of taking on supervisory positions, unless of course they work for one of the small number of firms, like the FI Group, which are built up around a home-based workforce. Conversely, teleworkers can find that their own managers are unhappy at the idea of supervising somebody whom they are unable personally to oversee.

It is also difficult for the home-based worker to keep up to date with the day-to-day social intercourse of work life: the opportunity to get to know your work colleagues better, for example, so that you can understand their particular interests and preoccupations – and know when to make allowances for the fact that they're having a bad day. Homeworkers are generally excluded from work gossip and chat, and are out of touch with the latest in office politics. You won't be able to eat in the office canteen, join other staff in social activities after work, or air your concerns so easily at union meetings.

There are various practical ways using new technology that the teleworker can communicate with work colleagues, as we shall see later. But the ordinary telephone is likely to be important in this process as well. Unfortunately, as every phone user knows, a telephone conversation is a poor substitute for a face-to-face meeting. Office-based colleagues may not understand the importance to a teleworker at home which a phone conversation can represent, as a substitute for ordinary office chat. Anxieties and fears ('Why was he so brusque today?...' Why wasn't she available to talk to me?') can build up unnecessarily.

Even the most sophisticated (and expensive) communications technology, such as videoconferencing, can't necessarily overcome these difficulties. It's hard to beat the advantages of meeting someone face-to-face.

It is clear, therefore, that you are unlikely to be bettering your chances of progressing up the normal career ladder by teleworking. But how much of a disadvantage is this for you? The question perhaps is whether success in purely orthodox career terms is what you want to achieve.

A related issue is that of work status. For many people, work provides not only an income but also a sense of purpose and self-fulfilment. The hazard of working at home is that the work you do will be taken less seriously by the outside world – and that in due course this external loss of status will challenge your sense of your own worth.

The process can be an insidious one. One home-based worker described for an American magazine what happened when she tried to book her child into a day nursery. 'They asked me whether I worked, and I said yes. Then they asked where, and I said at home,' she recounted. The response was upsetting: 'They acted like I didn't really work,' she said.

For senior executives, the opportunity to work from home can have the effect of enhancing their work status. But the situation for more junior staff, especially clerical workers, may be very different – particularly if there is a suspicion that pay levels are lower than for office-based staff.

Home-based work is likely to be experienced differently by men and women. As the authors of *Telework: Towards the Elusive Office* put it in a perceptive comment, 'the place of work is not normally regarded as gender-neutral. According to the prevailing stereotype, going out to work is experienced as a 'masculine' activity, while staying at home is seen as 'feminine'. This gives the act of going out to work, or not going out, quite a different meaning for men than for women.'.

Regrettably, domestic housework, as traditionally undertaken by women, is accorded less status in our society; power, status and money is to be found instead in the external world of the workplace. Women are perhaps more likely than men, therefore, to fear that teleworking will return them to the low-status role of being 'just' a stay-at-home housewife. Men are traditionally also less responsible than women for the day-to-day functioning of a household, and may find it easier to block out extraneous domestic interruptions – the pile of dirty washing, the blocked sink or the lack of anything in the fridge or freezer for dinner.

Self-discipline and work motivation

You're on your own. There is nobody to make you work, no external discipline to encourage you into a work frame of mind. There are no set hours of work. As a teleworker, you are responsible for establishing your own work discipline, and for creating your own rhythms for the working day.

According to some advocates, teleworking should be a way of allowing you to overcome the unnatural divide between work life and home life, and to achieve a more 'holistic' approach to life – or as the former SDP politician Shirley Williams put it, 'human beings can be made whole again, working and living in the same community'. But in reality, the divide between work and leisure-time remains, even for the home-based worker; indeed in some respects it is more important for a teleworker to acknowledge this, and to set aside definite periods of time for work.

In conventional working life commuting can even be an advantage, providing a barrier between work and home and offering the opportunity to adjust mentally at the beginning and end of each working day. Teleworkers do not have this facility – though there was a tale of a male home-based teleworker who left the front door of his house every morning dressed in a work suit, walked round the side of the building and reentered the house by a side door!

This seems a little extreme. But it can be helpful to develop regular start-of-day rituals – opening the mail, reading correspondence, or backing up computer files, perhaps. (This may also be the time to monitor your mailbox, if you use electronic mail – see page 88).

The discipline should work the other way, too. Just because you are never physically distant from your workplace doesn't mean that you shouldn't firmly shut away thoughts of work when the day's work is finished. As one enthusiast for the teleworking idea has warned: 'My wife and I are having a drink at the end of the day and the fax starts to clatter... it's just next door and I can hear it bloody clattering... I'm quite incapable of not going and lifting up the corner of the piece of paper...'.

Workaholism is a hazard. It can be sensible to decide, therefore, to attempt to work to regular hours. For some people, it may be appropriate to continue to work during normal office hours, beginning the day around nine and working until around five.

Teleworkers have a responsibility to themselves to look after other aspects of their health (we shall return to questions of health and safety in a later chapter). Establishing good work discipline means knowing when not to work. Exercise is important; for computer users, so is the practice of taking a regular 'screen break' from the monitor. And – though it may sound like a trivial remark – it is also sensible to guard against drinking too much coffee and tea, and against excessive eating. Several academic studies of teleworking have commented on the dangers of having too many snacks while at work: perhaps that idea of a remotely controlled locking fridge door may not be such a bad suggestion!

Space

As with time, so with space. A separation is needed between your work and leisure life, and this is much easier to achieve if a certain part of your house is dedicated as a work-space.

Of course, this is easier to achieve if you live in a house with a suitable spare room which can be converted into a proper study or office. But at the very least, a teleworker will need a part of a room where equipment and papers can be left undisturbed. Has your existing house got enough room for you to telework from it successfully?

'Perhaps a very "officey" office is needed to encourage the self-discipline needed when working at home,' argued one study of telework. One British furniture manufacturer, at least, appears to believe this is a market worth developing: the firm recently undertook a major magazine advertising campaign promoting 'the first fitted office furniture that doesn't look out of place in your home'.

A properly equipped study or office can help to prevent your work from encroaching into the rest of your house, and protect expensive electronic equipment from the dangers of being regularly moved, or – if there are children in the house – from being examined by inquisitive young fingers. It can also get round the sort of domestic problem faced by one teleworking computer programmer quoted in an issue of *Which?* magazine: 'My office is really the dining-room, and we need a couple of days' notice before having anyone to dinner!'

A separate workspace can also help to protect you from all-too-obvious domestic housework demands encroaching, so that you are shamed into vacuuming the living room carpet or tidying away the washing-up before you start the day's work. However, the use of part of your house exclusively for work raises certain tax issues, which you should take into account (see chapter 9).

Furniture needs some thought: there are good health reasons for ensuring, if you are using a computer, that you are not working too close to the monitor, and that the keyboard is positioned correctly to avoid repetitive strain injuries. A good office chair is not a luxury, if your long-term health depends on your posture at work. (We return to these questions in chapter 10.)

Location: where to telework

As we saw in the first chapter, in theory teleworkers may be able to base themselves anywhere they choose. However in practice there may be constraints – perhaps family reasons – which dictate where you are able to live. Arguably, too, it may be rash to combine a major change in your working life with all the stresses that can come from moving to a new home or a new area.

It may be necessary to remain within easy travelling distance of work colleagues or clients. Even if you're not commuting to work every day, you may still find that you need to attend meetings periodically. You may also decide that you want to keep in touch with work contacts by visiting them regularly in person.

In other words you may be dependent for your work not only on telecommunications links but also on transport links. If you *are* considering moving to a new location, it is sensible to research the road and rail links carefully, and if appropriate to check whether or not an airport can be reached easily. Likely travel costs should be taken into account when working out the financial implications of a move to teleworking.

The idea of living in the countryside is a powerful one for city-dwellers, and it is not surprising that many people have associated teleworking with the chance to leave city life behind. This attitude has been encouraged by a number of organisations concerned with rural affairs.

In northern Scotland, for example, Highlands and Islands Enterprise (formerly the Highlands and Islands Development Board) and British Telecom have jointly launched the 'Highlands and Islands Initiative', a multi-million pound investment programme in new digital telephone and telecom technology. Highlands and Islands Enterprise argues that by giving the north and west of Scotland the sort of high-quality telecommunications infrastructure that would normally only be found in large cities, their region can be compensated for its geographical remoteness. 'Information technology will unlock a huge field of commercial opportunities for the north of Scotland, and render distance from markets irrelevant', Sir Robert Cowan, chairman of the HIE, has said. 'Without doubt this is the most important single investment in the economic future of the Highlands and Islands.' Teleworking is one of the likely uses to which the new technology will be put, according to the HIE and BT.

In England, the organisation ACRE (the Association of Rural Community Councils in England) has taken an interest in the possibilities which teleworking could open up for country areas. In 1990, ACRE appointed a new Teleworking Advisor, Alan Denbigh, to develop this work. ACRE are currently producing an occasional newsletter on teleworking issues (see page 107).

The Rural Development Commission, the government appointed body with the task of overseeing economic activity in England's regional areas, has also taken an interest in the provision of telecommunications facilities in country areas.

However, while the dream of rural life can be delightful, it is as well not to confuse the image with the reality. As one officer with Highlands and Islands Enterprise put it, 'You're changing not only your house but also your lifestyle... People may have to travel 120 miles to their nearest Marks and Spencers!'.

Country living is not for everyone. The writer Piers Paul Read has described his own family's attempt to flee north from London to an eighteenth century farmhouse in Yorkshire. Originally, he says, it was the paradise they had expected. But gradually one or two snags emerged: 'The village was certainly secluded: we had to drive ten miles to fetch the newspaper. It was silent at night, but the day was regularly disturbed by the roar of low-flying jets. In summer this was joined by the throbbing motors of the combine harvesters.'.

Neither was the social life what he had been used to in London: 'Far from writing more because of the peace and quiet I found that boredom drove me to accept time-wasting appointments to bodies such as the Literature Panel of the Arts Council that paid my fare south. Tedium instead of distraction now paralysed my mind.' In due course, he and his family returned to city life.

The idea of 'living in the countryside' does no credit to the diversity of rural areas, and the enormous differences which can exist between villages, even those quite close to each other geographically. If you can, it's a good idea to get to know an area – out-of-season in the winter months as well as in summer – before you take the plunge. Remember that the lower the population density and the more remote the area, the smaller the local social and economic network will be:

you are likely to have to travel further to get what you need. Facilities that town-dwellers take for granted – schools, shops, social amenities – and services which you may need to call on – doctors, car mechanics and computer repairers – will not necessarily be available on your doorstep.

There are also technical aspects to bear in mind if you are contemplating teleworking from a rural area. For example, how reliable will your telephone service be, if the telephone wires run several miles across open moorland to reach your cottage? Can you rely on a trouble-free supply of electricity to run your computer equipment? (At the very least, invest a few pounds in a 'surge plug', to iron out surges and spikes in the supply.)

British Telecom's transformation from a state-run service to a commercial business has been regulated by the terms of its operational licence, overseen by the government watchdog Oftel. Among other things, this has meant that, so far, BT has been obliged to continue the policy of uniform charging, so that services to remote rural areas are normally supplied at the same tariff as applying to built-up city areas. However, already there has been one move in the direction of 'deaveraging' (that is, charging different customers different prices for the same service): this has been BT's introduction of low-cost 'b1' trunk routes between major centres of population.

Any future moves towards 'deaveraging' could penalise telephone users in less well-populated areas. In any case, rural users already face the fact that they can reach fewer other phone subscribers at local charge rates than city users. For example, London telephone users can contact more than three million other subscribers for the price of a local call; Cornish subscribers can reach around 100,000 users.

The rival telephone service from Mercury is currently not available to all areas of Britain; Mercury have quite naturally concentrated on laying down trunk routes between the main centres of population. The Rural Development Commission and Oftel, in a 1989 study, conclude: 'It is clear that local service in the rural areas is likely to be the monopoly of BT in the foreseeable future.'. Their study also points out that other newer forms of telecommunication, such as Cellnet and

Vodafone mobile telephone services and radiopaging, do not reach all parts of the country.

Would-be teleworkers planning a very remote lifestyle should also be aware of BT's existing '100 hours' rule. This lays down that BT is permitted to charge the full cost of installing a telephone connection in cases where more than 100 hours of worktime are involved. In fairness it should perhaps be added that it is rare for BT to invoke this rule.

Children, childcare

When the Geneva-based International Labour Office produced an international survey of teleworking in 1990, they chose to reflect the subject matter with a cover photograph, showing a (male) teleworker hard at work at his personal computer. Just to his side in the photograph was a baby, sitting in a high chair and cheerfully playing with a collection of toys. The baby's feeding bottle was perched close at hand, just next to the computer keyboard.

It was obviously a posed shot: but the photograph nonetheless sums up the widely held view that teleworking is particularly suitable for those with children to look after. Work and home life can be reintegrated, and the responsibilities of childcare reconciled with the needs and pleasures of work. This can mean, to use Shirley Williams' phrase once more, that 'human beings can be made whole again'.

Most parents who go out to work mourn the fact that they can spend so little time with their children. Most working parents also know the problems of trying to arrange childcare, and of making sure that someone is available to cope, for example, with school holidays or when their children are unwell. It is mainly women who in practice carry much of this responsibility.

Teleworking can be the answer, it's claimed. It is significant that studies have shown that a large percentage of teleworkers are women with young children. One researcher has reported that women teleworkers in his survey 'were able to attain a rounded and holistic existence working and mothering as they pleased'.

Combining work and childcare is a wonderfully attractive idea. But is it all too good to be true? The day-to-day routine of an American woman Sandra Larkin, as reported in a magazine article in 1987, might give pause for thought. Her work, as as a paste-up editor for a Chicago publisher, was fitted in around childcare, so that during a typical day she began work at about 7.30am, working for a couple of hours until 9.30am. She then attended to her family and home responsibilities, recommencing work in the evening at about 8.30pm-9pm amd working on to into the early hours, finally finishing work as late as 2am.

The author of that article, Kathleen Christensen, has also described the experience of another teleworker, who came to an arrangement to work for a set number of hours a day in an upstairs office while her child was looked after by a childminder downstairs: 'Although she has the benefit of strict spatial and temporal boundaries between work and family, she is not exempt from conflict. She feels torn and guilty hearing her son cry... Often she covers her ears or puts on ear phones so as not to jump up and rush downstairs.'.

This doesn't sound much like a rounded or holistic existence. The reality, surely, is that it is just not possible to assume that you can work full-time at home while caring for a young child at the same time.

But what telework can perhaps offer for those with childcare responsibilities is greater flexibility. If you are controlling your own hours of work, and if you are no longer dependent on a lengthy journey in to your workplace, it's easier to vary your work schedule and to switch back as needed into your parental role. Time can be taken off to take your child to the clinic or to a dentist's appointment, or to see them perform in the school assembly, for example. Illnesses may no longer be quite so difficult to cope with. You may be able to plan your work to fit in better with nursery or school hours.

However, for most teleworkers some form of organised childcare arrangement will be essential – and of course may well involve regular expense. Employees who are switching from working at an employer's premises to working from home may be penalised, if the employer has provided a workplace nursery: under changes announced in the 1990 Budget, income tax relief is available for workplace nurseries, but not from costs involved in other child care arrangements. This is an area where childcare organisations are campaigning for the rules to be changed, and the tax relief extended.

Family relationships

What will be the effect on other members of your family, if you decide to begin working from home? How, in particular, will the relationship with your partner be affected, if you are married or living with another person?

Alvin Toffler, as we saw in the last chapter, has graphically described his vision of life in the future in the electronic cottage in his book *The Third Wave*. But when it comes to considering what effects this could have on personal relationships, he carefully keeps his options open:

> 'Relocating work into the home means that many spouses who now see each other only a limited number of hours each day could be thrown together more intimately. Some, no doubt, would find this prolonged proximity hateful. Many others, however, would find their marriages saved and their relationships much enriched through shared experience.'

Rank Xerox, when they initiated their teleworking experiment in the early 1980s, made it a condition that not only the prospective teleworker but also their spouse completed a short psychological test, set by a career analysis company, to assess their suitability for this way of working. The spouse had to agree to the teleworking proposal before it went ahead. (This approach could be construed depending on your point of view either as good personnel practice, showing a commendable concern for employees' future welfare, or as an unjustified intrusion into employees' private lives.)

In fact, in this as in other areas, women teleworkers are likely to experience the issues rather differently from male teleworkers. The effect which a move to teleworking has on personal relationships is also likely to depend very much on whether both partners will be at home during working hours, or whether one will continue to go out to work.

There is perhaps a danger, if one partner works from home while the other continues to work away from the house, that the teleworker will have to take on greater domestic responsibilities. It probably makes sense for the partner at home to open the door for the gas meter reader, arrange a time for the plumber to call when the drains are blocked or ring the council when the bins aren't emptied. Whether it is also fair to expect the partner working at home to take more responsibility for the shopping, cleaning or cooking is perhaps another question. A woman teleworker in particular might find it hard to resist the feeling that these are all tasks she should take on board; men, who have traditionally played less of a role in household management, might find it easier to concentrate blithely just on their 'real' work.

Other issues arise where both partners are at home. In circumstances where men and women have previously shared responsibilities in a traditional way, with the man leaving home for waged work while the woman remained to attend to housework and family, it is clear that there can be problems when this arrangement is changed for any reason. Women whose partners become unemployed or who reach retirement age have to adjust to the fact that they no longer have the house to themselves during daytime hours and that, whilst they may be busy, their partners may have excess time to kill. It can be a time of painful adjustment for both people.

If the man is returning to the house to telework, he will at least not have the problem of enforced idleness. However, his partner may feel an obligation to service her partner during the working day – by making cups of coffee and regular midday meals, for example, or perhaps answering the telephone. The previous flexibility she had in working out her day's activities may begin to disappear.

There are issues here for families to discuss, before the decision is taken to move to teleworking. It would be nice to think that, by talking things through beforehand, partners do indeed find, as Toffler suggests, that their relationships are enriched by the experience.

Financial and employment implications

How will your personal finances be affected by a decision to stop commuting to work and start teleworking?

There are a number of obvious savings which you may be able to make, most directly in the costs of travelling to and from your workplace, and including perhaps car parking expenses; you may also be able to save much of the expense of midday meals at work and of having to buy expensive clothing, such as business suits.

As we saw in the last chapter, teleworking may save companies money as well. To some extent, their savings may be real economies that come simply from the change in work organisation. But it may also be that the savings are at the expense of the teleworker. As the 1982 Equal Opportunities Commission survey (see page 14) suggested, wage levels for teleworkers can frequently be lower than for office-based staff.

It may also be that the employer is able to transfer some overheads to the teleworker: this could include anything from the cost of minor items like office biros and notebooks to more substantial expenditure, such as the cost of maintaining the work premises. Who will be paying for the cost of heating, lighting and cleaning the home office? What about important issues like maintenance contracts on capital items like computers and insurance? Indeed, is the employer going to be supplying all the necessary capital equipment, including suitable office desks and chairs, or will the teleworker be using his or her own property?

When you are office based, the odd day worked at home to catch up on your work reading, for example, is unlikely to leave you out of pocket. But if your home becomes your full-time workplace, there are longer term financial implications. Your carpets will wear out quicker, the paintwork and wallpaper get tattier – and of course your telephone bill will increase considerably.

There will also be obvious expenses involved if you move house – if perhaps your present house is not large enough to enable you to telework from it. Even if you have already got space to convert to an office, however, there will be actual or implicit costs involved – you will be losing a room of your house which could be generating income from a lodger or from bed and breakfast visitors, or which at least could be used for other non-work activities. Will you be compensated for the fact that your business is effectively 'renting' space in your home?

The Equal Opportunities Commission report concluded with a 'code of good practice' which it suggests employers should follow when using homeworkers. It may be useful at this point to summarise the points it makes:

- Anyone working at home primarily for one employer should be given full employee status
- Home-based employees should receive the same rates of pay as on-site employees, including overtime and unsocial hours payments
- All expenses should be paid
- Employers should try to help reduce homeworkers' social isolation
- Employers should keep homeworkers informed of new developments in the organisation; homeworkers should be training opportunities
- Career paths should be kept open
- Homeworkers wishing to return on-site should be able to do so
- Homeworkers should be informed of other vacancies in the organisation
- Homeworking should be counted as continuous employment with any previous on-site work
- The employer should supply all necessary equipment
- Appropriate trade unions should be given the means to contact homeworkers

If you are thinking of combining teleworking with a move to self-employment, the implications – financial and otherwise – are much greater. As we saw with the examples of California Western States Life and Rank Xerox, some companies have linked telework with an attempt to sever their legal employment responsibilities to former members of staff. This amounts in effect to a situation of voluntary redundancy, and it has major repercussions for the individual.

Self-employed people do not have many of the rights enjoyed by employees. These are likely to include, apart from a guaranteed wage packet: holiday entitlement, sick pay provision, maternity rights, protection from unfair dismissal, and perhaps participation in an occupational pension scheme. The employer also pays a considerable share of the employee's National Insurance contributions.

On the other hand, there can be benefits to self-employment, and not just the pleasure of being your own boss. The tax treatment of the self-employed is very different from the Pay As You Earn system, and in some instances is more generous. An accountant, or indeed one of the many books available on running your own business, will be able to give you more details. Self-employed individuals are responsible for paying their own National Insurance contributions (Class 2, and if profits are sufficiently high, Class 4); however the self-employed are not entitled to the full range of N.I. contribution-linked benefits, including unemployment benefit.

One implication of becoming self-employed, therefore, is that you should consider carefully what insurance you will need, including perhaps an income protection policy in the case of prolonged illness. You will also be responsible for your own pension.

If your turnover is over the VAT threshold (£35,000 for the year 1991/2) you will be required to register for VAT. If your turnover if below this, it may still be worth seeking voluntary registration, particularly if most of your clients are themselves VAT registered, so that you will be able to reclaim VAT on your business expenses.

If you are running your own business, you also have an additional choice of opting to create your own limited company; this has the effect of separating your business finances entirely from your personal finances. As a director of the company, you would once again revert to employee status in tax terms. Professional advice is necessary if you feel that this legal structure may be appropriate in your situation.

In some circumstances, the dividing line between being self-employed and being an employee is hard to define. Even if you consider yourself self-employed, it is open to the Inland Revenue to assert that you are in reality an employee - and for them to attempt to reclaim (normally from your alleged 'employer') any Pay As You

Earn contributions they claim should have been paid. This is an area we consider in Chapter 9.

If you are contemplating beginning a new business by teleworking from a country area bear in mind that various forms of government assistance, including grants and loans, are available to rural-based businesses. In England the government organisation responsible is the Rural Development Commission. The RDC's Redundant Building Grant scheme offers grants for the conversion of unused rural buildings into business premises; grants are for 25% of the total conversion cost, and are restricted to the RDC's priority areas, the so-called Rural Development Areas. The RDC also makes loans available in some circumstances for rural-based businesses. The RDC has a network of local offices, with staff who are normally happy to offer advice to small businesses in their area.

In Scotland, there are a number of different schemes to assist small business; contact Scottish Enterprise for details. Highlands and Islands Enterprise covers the north and west of the country, from Argyll to Shetland. In Wales, responsibility is split between the Welsh Development Agency (roughly north and south Wales) and the Development Board for Rural Wales (roughly mid-Wales).

INFORMATION

Rural Development Commission, 11 Cowley Street, London SW1P 3NA. Tel: 071 276 6969; and 141 Castle Street, Salisbury, Wilts SP1 3TP. Tel: 0722 336255
Small Business Advisory Service, Scottish Enterprise, 21 Bothwell St, Glasgow G2 6NR. Tel: 041 248 6014
Highlands and Islands Enterprise, Bridge House, 20 Bridge St, Inverness IV1 1QR. Tel: 0463 234171
Welsh Development Agency, Pearl House, Greyfriars Rd, Cardiff CF1 3XX. Tel: 0222 222666
The Development Board for Rural Wales, Ladywell House, Newtown, Powys SY16 1JB. Tel: 0686 626965 or freephone 0800 269300

Longer-term implications

To conclude this chapter, it is appropriate to look briefly at some of the possible longer-term implications of deciding to telework.

A traditional office-based job is likely to have implicit within it the possibilities of change and development: the potential, perhaps, of promotion, and of taking on new responsibilities. Training in new skills – and in new technology – may also be readily available. By contrast, teleworkers may not feel that they have the same opportunities to develop; work towards new targets or challenges will have to be self-motivated.

Tom Forester teleworked as a full-time writer for seven years, and has described his experiences as following 'a familiar pattern: an initial honeymoon period of two to three years, which was accompanied by feelings of elation and high productivity, was followed by a less satisfactory period which was accompanied by feelings of loneliness, isolation and a growing desire to escape the "same four walls".' Eventually he decided to take a three-days-a-week conventional job.

As in other areas of life, the teleworker needs to guard against burnout. Loneliness and isolation can also be demoralising. The problem here is perhaps not the obvious one that nobody else is physically working in the same office as you: it is more to do with the fact that nobody else is necessarily aware of the work you are doing or is concerned with how you are getting on.

It is also possible that, by being away from the office environment, you miss out on the chance to see how your own work fits in with other people's. You might find, for example, that you spend your days editing the text of company reports without ever having the opportunity to see the finished result.

One teleworker interviewed for the Equal Opportunities Commission study reported that 'when she got really desperate she coped by getting into her car and driving fourteen miles to see a colleague who was also a homeworker'. As we shall see in chapter 10, there are a number of self-help organisations, most notably OwnBase, which have been set up by and for home-based workers, to share experiences and to combat isolation. Some teleworkers also find that on-line bulletin boards (see page 91) are an effective electronic way of keeping in touch with others.

Further information

A list of a number of books and journal articles on telework is included in Appendix 2.

British Telecom have produced an introductory booklet, available free of charge, designed to provide information for teleworkers:

INFORMATION

A Guide to Working from Home; published British Telecom. Available on request; Tel: 0800 800878

4
TELEWORK AND THE TELEPHONE

The letters page of *The Independent* one day in early 1991 carried this rueful observation from one of its readers: 'Last night I was awakened by two telephone calls, the first at 1am and the second at 3am, to hear, on blearily lifting the handset, what I now know to be a fax machine whining..

'I have no fax machine, my old-fashioned telephone works only on normal voice exchange. Do any readers have a suggestion for what words, or indeed what sounds, I might send down my telephone to dissuade this errant fax from disturbing me further?' Failing that, the letter continued, 'would all those sending faxes from (I deduce from the time of night) Japan or Australasia to Welwyn Garden City please check the numbers they are using?'.

The telephone service is changing fast. The days when a phone was simply a phone and could be used just for 'old-fashioned' ordinary voice conversations have gone. All sorts of devices now come with telephone jacks attached (whilst the letter-writer above assumed that he was dealing with a fax machine – understandably given the popularity which facsimile transmission has now acquired – his nocturnal intruder could as easily have been a computer).

What has happened over the past few years is that computer and telecommunications technologies have begun to coalesce. Where once there were two distinct industries there is now a new hybrid, loosely described by the term Information Technology. We shall consider in the following chapters the way in which computers – including the cheapest personal computers – can be hooked into the telephone network, and the profound practical implications this has for home-based teleworkers. But first it is necessary to consider the changes that have been happening to the telephone service since British Telecom was denationalised in 1984, and to look ahead at the new services likely to be available later in the 1990s.

The changes have been two-fold: not only technological but also regulatory. Although many people have perhaps yet to register the fact, the British telephone service is no longer synonymous with BT. The post-privatisation regulation of the telephone supply industry involved the creation of an element of competition, with Mercury (part of the Cable and Wireless Group) allowed to challenge BT for business. It has admittedly been a very one-sided duopoly, with BT still dominant in most areas. Mercury has had to build up its own alternative telephone network, but has now reached the point where the company claims that about 75% of the population is able to use its services. This means, for example, that you can opt to have your long-distance telephone calls sent on the Mercury network rather than down BT's lines (BT continue to own the local telephone lines, but are obliged to carry Mercury's calls on the first and last legs of their journey). At present BT have an effective monopoly on local calls.

However, the government is now considering changing the rules again, to allow other organisations to offer telephone services. The BT/Mercury duopoly is to go, and such apparently unlikely concerns as British Rail may soon be competing with BT and Mercury.

The government's plans were set out in a white paper published in March 1991. This presents a wide range of proposals for the future regulation of telecommunications provision in Britain, which – if implemented – would involve significant changes. Among other things, the government proposes to allow other companies to offer to carry long-distance telephone calls. There are already a number of extensive private telecommunications networks in existence, which could relatively easily be converted to public use. This is the reason why British Rail, for example, is involved: it has already set up a subsidiary, British Rail Telecommunications, to consider ways of developing and marketing its own national communications network. BR are talking of copying Mercury's 'blue phones' with their own 'green phones'. Other organisations who are currently investigating this sort of telephone service include the electricity supply companies, British Waterways and the Independent Broadcasting Authority.

The cable TV companies who have been busy wiring up many of Britain's cities over the past decade are also likely to be involved, since the cables which bring TV pictures into their subscribers' homes can easily be used in addition for sending and receiving telephone calls. Already some cable TV companies are offering limited phone services: at present, the cable companies are acting as local agents for Mercury, feeding customers into Mercury's trunk network. However, the government's white paper proposes to allow cable companies to offer telephone services in their own right. Cable companies may soon be in a position, therefore, to compete with BT in providing comprehensive local telephone services.

A time may come, in fact, when the telecommunications and broadcasting networks are much more closely integrated. The same modern telecommunications infrastructure can be used for providing both telephone and television services – and a whole range of other business-related and entertainment facilities. For the present, however, the government has decided to prohibit BT and Mercury from offering television services through their networks: the idea is to encourage the cable TV companies to continue with their investment programmes.

BT is currently the 'natural' supplier of telephone services, in that you have to make a conscious decision – by obtaining a Mercury ID, and investing in a Mercury-compatible telephone – to have the choice of routing your calls other than by BT. But the government plans changes here as well, and wants to create what it calls 'equal access'. John Redwood, a junior minister in the Department of Trade and Industry, has described his government's plans as follows:

> 'At the moment you need a separate blue button phone in order to be able to use either BT or Mercury's trunk lines. In phase one of equal access it will be possible to pre-select using your existing phone the trunk carrier you wish to use. In the second phase of equal access, using your ordinary phone at home, it will be possible by dialling just two additional digits to choose the operator you want for each trunk call on a call by call basis. Systems may also develop offering people a way of making the choice automatically to provide them with the quickest and cheapest routing for their calls.'

For the teleworker, more reliant on an efficient and cheap phone service than most people, this extension of competition may seem encouraging. However, it is less clear how easy it will be to get the information you will need in order to make sensible choices between competing services. The experience of the mobile phone business in recent years suggests that choosing the best deal can be a tricky and time-consuming business.

Mobile phone services are themselves changing, the main development here being the arrival of the more sophisticated Personal Communications Networks in the next few years. PCNs are the second generation of mobile communication. Like the existing mobile phone service (where Cellnet and Vodafone are the two licensed operators), PCNs will be structured on a cell basis, with radio connections to the normal telephone network from each cell. Your call is automatically switched between transmitters as you move from one cell area to another.

There are three companies who have been licensed by the government to develop PCNs: a consortium headed by Mercury, another led by British Aerospace and a third with major US and German telecommunication interests, Unitel Ltd. PCNs will be based on a different radio frequency spectrum to the existing Cellnet and Vodafone services, which will mean that the country will have to blanketed with a much larger number of cells, but which should also mean better quality reception and less congestion. PCNs will have capacity for up to twelve million subscribers: to fulfil the potential and repay the initial investment, therefore, PCN operators are likely to attempt to break into the mass marketplace.

PCN services are expected to be introduced from late 1992 onwards, initially in city areas. However, 'by the mid to late 1990s, the cost and convenience of equipment may make the use of a PCN a competitive alternative not only to the cellular operators' services but also to the fixed telephone network,' according to the Department of Trade and Industry. There will also be technical compatibility with western European cellular radio telephone services.

With a profusion of new telephone service suppliers and with the forthcoming arrival of PCNs something obviously has got to be done to ensure that there is a sensible policy over the issuing of telephone numbers; in fact, the government's regulatory body, Oftel, has taken responsibility for this. It is clear that there could be major changes in the future. One idea which may soon be technically feasible is for each telephone subscriber to be given a personal telephone number for life, which they will be able to take with them as they move house, and which will also be usable on any mobile phone equipment they may have.

The exact regulatory framework for telephone services in the later 1990s depends on whether the 1991 white paper proposals are converted into legislation, or whether they are revised (a likelihood if a Labour government is elected). However, the technical changes which have been transforming the telecommunications industry are equally dramatic, if less obvious to ordinary phone subscribers.

The traditional telephone network has worked on analogue principles: that is, the signals have been sent to and fro in wave form. What is happening at the moment is that the old analogue network is gradually being replaced by digital technology. A digital telephone network operates by converting the messages being sent – whether speech, data, pictures or other information – into a number of on-off pulses. (This is of course similar to the way that data is processed and stored electronically by computers.) About half Britain's telephone exchanges are now digital.

There are a number of benefits of using digital technology. Phone calls can be routed through exchange switching mechanisms much more quickly and reliably, for example. Digital networks offer the potential of direct computer communication, without the need for signals to be converted into analogue through a 'modem' (see chapter 5).

Some telephone subscribers are already able to link up to the so-called Integrated Services Digital Network (ISDN), a comprehensive combined telecommunications network capable of handling not only voice phone calls but many other more sophisticated kinds of information exchange at extremely fast speeds of transmission. A single page fax transmission for example can take just two seconds when sent through ISDN.

What do all these changes mean in practice for the teleworker? The rest of this chapter looks at a number of telephone related services which may be useful when teleworking. There are details of where to get further information.

Telephone service providers

As we have seen, only BT and Mercury are currently licensed as public telephone operators. For ordinary telephone users, a BT line is essential, even if Mercury is chosen additionally for use when calling long-distance.

BT distinguish between residential and business users. Business subscribers pay more (currently about £30 plus VAT extra for initial connection, and about £10 more per quarter). In exchange, they are offered a better line quicker repair service and a slightly faster installation time; there are other possible advantages, such as inclusion in Yellow Pages.

Teleworkers are in an unusual position in effectively being able to choose whether to set up a residential or business line.

BT's tariffs changed in September 1991 with a range of pricing packages offered, including for the first time an automatic volume discount for heavy telephone users.

INFORMATION

Contact British Telecom via the operator. Dial 100 and ask for Freefone Telecom Sales

Mercury claim that, at present, they are cheaper than BT for long distance calls (i.e., calls beyond the local charge area). They say that in general customers who make a number of long distance calls can save 'substantially' on their total phone bill.

Not everybody is able to use Mercury: one in four exchanges are not yet linked up. To find out whether your exchange is covered, contact Mercury Customer Assistance.

Mercury charge a small annual fee (currently £7.50 plus VAT) for use of the necessary ID. To use Mercury, you will normally need a

Mercury-compatible phone (one with a blue button which you press, when you want to route your call over Mercury's lines). These phones are available in large electrical stores, and cost from about £25.

Alternatively, it is possible to use a Mercury 'smart socket' with an ordinary telephone; this acts as a buffer between your phone and the master socket, automatically routing calls via Mercury if it detects they are long-distance. Smart sockets are manufactured by a firm called Intercom, and currently cost £99.99 including VAT.

INFORMATION

Mercury Customer Assistance, PO Box 49, Birmingham B1 1TE. Phone freephone 0800 424194.
Intercom have a freephone number, 0800 626474

BT and Mercury operate under the conditions imposed by the regulatory body, the Office of Telecommunications (Oftel). Oftel have a consumer department, where enquiries or complaints from the public about telephone service provision are handled. Oftel also produce a wide range of booklets on issues related to telecommunications regulation.

INFORMATION

Office of Telecommunications, Export House, 50 Ludgate Hill,
London EC4M 7JJ. Tel: 071 822 1600

LinkLines

The familiar 0800 freephone service, together with 0345 numbers where callers are charged at local call rates regardless of distance, are jointly marketed by BT as 'LinkLines'. 'Freefone' provides a similar service to the 0800 lines through the operator. BT also offer a Call Forwarding facility, where calls to one number are automatically forwarded to a number elsewhere.

These services are by no means cheap, though BT have recently revised their prices, so that it is possible to rent a LinkLine for £200 a year (plus £250 connection). In certain circumstances, teleworkers might consider them worth the expense. The Rural Development Commission report the case of one mortgage broker living in Cornwall but generating 'local' business from his previous town in the Home Counties through the use of a LinkLine 0800 number and a Post Office box number. LinkLines and call forwarding offer a way for teleworkers not to have to reveal to business clients where they are based geographically – useful perhaps if it is psychologically important for your business to give the impression of being run from metropolitan London even when in reality you are working from your home in Wester Ross!

Answering facilities and paging

Answering machines can be bought for little more than £50, or as much as £250. Most models include some form of remote control, so that you can monitor messages while away from your desk.

INFORMATION

Which? magazine reviewed answering machines in its August 1990 issue

BT, Mercury and others provide various paging services. The pagers range from simple tone alerts to full message displays.

INFORMATION

BT offer brochures on their paging services which can be ordered by telephoning 0800 222611

BT also operate a sophisticated 'voicemail' service known as VoiceBank. At its simplest this can be treated just as a computerised remote-control answerphone, although it is in effect a voice equivalent of an electronic mail service. Like e-mail (see page 88), you can check your personal 'mailbox' for messages left for you, and can then delete them, save them on the host computer or even forward them to other VoiceBank subscribers.

BT claim perhaps a little unconvincingly that VoiceBank could be useful when combined with a pager or mobile phone, or for internal use for exchanging messages between staff in a large organisation. VoiceBank operates from a separate number from your ordinary telephone.

INFORMATION

BT have a freephone number, 0800 222677

Another company which offers a voicemail facility, as one part of a package of its 'intelligent telephony' services, is Telecom Express Ltd.

INFORMATION

Telecom Express Ltd, 211 Piccadilly, London W1 Tel: 071 412 0412

Services from digital exchanges

Subscribers whose telephone exchanges are digital have the opportunity to use a number of additional features, formerly marketed by BT as 'star services' and more recently renamed 'network services'. They include:

- charge advice (you are told after a call what it has cost)
- call diversion (redirects a call to a programmed alternative number)
- call waiting (informs you by means of a discrete bleep when you are on the telephone that another caller is trying to reach you; you can then put your first call on hold while you answer the second call)
- three-way calling (a mini conferencing facility)
- call barring
- short code dialling for regularly used numbers
- reminder call (telephone used as form of alarm clock)

These services, which are relatively inexpensive, point the way to the types of service which are likely to become increasingly commonplace. Some similar services are available for Mercury subscribers using cable television access.

INFORMATION

BT subscribers: ring 100 and ask for FreeFone Telecom Sales

Videoconferencing

Video telephones are still in their infancy. However, BT has a network of seven public videoconferencing studios in Britain which can be hired for short periods, as a substitute for face-to-face meetings. The studios are situated in London, Edinburgh, Glasgow, Manchester, Birmingham, Bristol and the Isle of Man. The studios are small rooms with a table and chairs for up to six people who sit facing two video screens opposite them. When in use, these screens show the images of other conference participants, who will be sitting in a similar studio elsewhere in the country.

Studios can be booked for periods of 30 minutes upwards, and BT say that the costs typically begin at £100-£200 per hour for a UK conference. International videoconferencing is also possible to the USA, Japan and a number of western European countries.

INFORMATION

BT have a freephone number 0800 282282

Mobile communications

'One of the great scourges of modern life': this was the phrase the Chancellor of the Exchequer used during his 1991 Budget speech to describe the mobile phone (he went on to impose a £200 tax liability for business mobile phones used for private purposes).

However, there are now many hundreds of thousands of users of cellular phones in Britain who would presumably disagree with the Chancellor's assessment. Britain leads the rest of western Europe in the usage of mobile phones, and as we saw above the introduction from 1992 of the next generation of cellular phones, Personal Communications Networks (PCNs), may increase their popularity further.

Mobile phones allow the user to communicate with ordinary BT telephones, or with other mobile phones; they can also be used in conjunction with portable fax machines, or with portable computers equipped with modems. In principle, this could mean that you could choose to telework from wherever you pleased, outdoors or indoors, stationary or on the move – provided that you remained within reach of one of the cellular base stations. Currently, however, the cellular services can suffer from congestion and technical shortcomings, such as background noise and dropped calls.

There are two competing cellular telephone services, run by Cellnet (in which BT is the majority partner) and Vodafone. However, neither company is currently allowed by the government to sell its services directly to the public. (This restriction will be removed at the end of 1992.) Instead, you have to deal with an intermediary, a 'service provider': it is this service provider who will bill you, and with whom you sign a contract. In theory, you should be able to have a service provider of your choice; however some portable phone retailers may attempt to steer you towards one particular company. A *Which?* magazine report in April 1991 was critical of certain contractual conditions imposed by some service providers, and advised readers to shop around between companies. *Which?* also disclosed that, in a survey it had carried out, Vodafone had generally proved more technically reliable than Cellnet.

The phones themselves may be fully hand-portable, 'transportable' (equipped with a battery pack) or permanently installed in a car (running off a car battery). Prices have dropped; however, a mobile phone installed in a car is still likely to cost up to £250, including installation. Hand portables generally cost more. You will also have to pay the rental costs of the phone (typically £25 a month plus VAT), and the call charges for all calls you make (typically up to 38p a minute).

INFORMATION

Cellnet and Vodafone provide information and lists of service providers:
Cellnet: 0800 424323
Vodafone Marketing department: 0635 503292

Oftel produce a useful booklet about mobile phones
Office of Telecommunications, Export House, 50 Ludgate Hill, London EC4M 7JJ.
Tel: 071 822 1600

An alternative to fully mobile phones is the cordless telephone service, generically known as Telepoint or CT2. Telepoint allows you to make calls (although not currently receive them), provided you are within radio transmission distance (about 100 yards) of a Telepoint base – such places as motorway service stations or railway stations, for example. Confusingly, four licensed operators were authorised to operate Telepoint services, each of whom was expected to have its own pricing structure and separate brand name. It hasn't worked out like that. Mercury (operating 'Callpoint') recently decided to pull out of the market; Ferranti have also suspended their 'Zonepoint' service and are reported to be searching for a buyer. A third Telepoint operating service has yet to be launched. That leaves just BT, with its service known as Phonepoint.

Telepoint is certainly cheaper than a full cellular service, but much less flexible. To date, the service has attracted only a relative handful of subscribers.

Fax

It is appropriate to end this chapter as we began, with a brief look at facsimile (fax) transmission. What a few years ago was an exotic piece of technology has now become widely used, and almost as valuable for many businesses as ordinary telephone communication. Prices for basic fax machines have fallen considerably in recent years, and are still falling.

Fax transmission allows you to send and receive documents over a telephone line; the documents can be typed, handwritten or consist of drawings or photographs. A fax machine is made up of a scanner, a modem and a printer – as you feed a document into your machine for transmission, the image on the paper is broken down into a large number of extremely small rectangles, which are scanned to determine whether they are black or white. This digitalised information is converted by the internal modem into a form which can be transmitted through the telephone network. Incoming faxes get the same treatment in reverse, before being sent to the printer. Most fax machines have thermal printers, which mean that you have to buy rolls of heat sensitive paper. In time, documents on this paper may begin to fade. Some more recent fax machines print on to ordinary paper.

Many people choose to install a second telephone line to handle fax transmission, although if necessary fax machines can be plugged in to the same line as an ordinary telephone. Obviously, you won't be able to use the fax machine at the same time as using the phone. There can be a problem in dealing with incoming calls when you are unable to answer the phone personally. A phone/fax switching device can be purchased for about £90, or you can buy a combined fax and answering machine, which automatically distinguishes fax calls from ordinary voice messages. If you do install a separate line dedicated for fax transmission, it is probably better not to publicise the number in a directory: 'junk' fax mail can be a problem, and it is your expensive heat sensitive paper which is being used to print out the unwanted messages.

The vast majority of current fax machines are 'class 3' machines. Technical standards have already been worked out for the forthcoming class 4 machines, though it will be some years before these are widely available.

Fax machines replicate many of the features which you may already have on your personal computer system; one alternative to an ordinary fax machine, therefore, is to upgrade your PC by installing a fax-card. This is normally relatively easy to fit. However, unless you splash out in addition on a scanner, you will only be able to send plain text (ASCII) files, or graphics produced by a small number of graphics software packages. Incoming faxes will be saved and can be printed out; however they cannot normally be directly converted into files for subsequent word processing.

Subscribers to electronic mail services (see page 88) are able to send plain text messages to fax (and indeed telex) machines direct from their computer, without the need for their own fax machine or fax-card; however, incoming faxes cannot currently be received through electronic mail.

The widespread use of fax is encouraging a growing number of companies to develop commercial information services using the fax machine as a delivery mechanism for supplying details requested by the user. As early as 1988 the TSB showed what was possible by offering its banking customers the chance to order instant bank statements, forwarded straight to their fax machine. The system is completely computerised, and involves the customer giving instructions, using a keypad, direct to the bank's mainframe computer.

Mercury recently launched a similar facility, marketed as Faxess. This was put to use during the Gulf War by the US Embassy to push out its press releases to journalists; journalists were able to choose by telephone what information they were interested in receiving, and the press releases then duly slipped out of their fax machines moments later. Again the system was fully computerised.

Mercury are providing the Faxess technology, but are not themselves taking on the role of information provider; however they say that they expect a company information service, offering details about individual limited companies by fax, to start up soon. (As we shall see in a later chapter, this sort of information is already available from on-line computer database services).

Mercury have something of an edge in this area at present but other companies are also exploring ways to develop similar services. One company is Telecom Express Ltd (see address above), who have also developed a fax messaging facility; this enables incoming faxes to be held on a central computer until such time as the recipient asks to see them. Faxes can be redirected or forwarded to any other fax machine number requested.

INFORMATION

A survey by *Which?* magazine of fax machines was carried in the August 1990 issue

5
GOING ON-LINE: AN INTRODUCTION TO COMPUTER COMMUNICATIONS

When the concept of teleworking was first mooted in the 'Seventies, it was assumed that home-based workers would be working at simple terminals, linked up through data communications channels with distant mainframes which would be doing all the actual computing work.

The arrival of microcomputers has changed all that. Teleworkers can now equip themselves with their own independent computing power (and year by year microcomputers become ever faster and more powerful, and the software available ever more sophisticated).

But even if as a teleworker you are no longer obliged to rely on data links to computers elsewhere, it still makes good sense to explore the potential which comes from linking your computer up to others. By simply connecting your computer into the ordinary telephone network you can go 'on-line': that is, you can reach other computers worldwide, transferring information backwards and forwards at will. As we shall see in the next few chapters, there is a vast choice of on-line services available, providing access both to information (of all kinds) and to new means of communication.

Attempting to go on-line for the first time, however, can seem a little daunting. The world of computer communications ('comms') is still heavily larded with technical terminology – words like baud, duplex, parity and protocol which don't normally figure (at least in the sense they mean here) in most people's vocabulary.

Don't be daunted. Simply keep in mind that your telephone line can carry information to and from your computer as easily as it can carry ordinary voice conversations.

Phone calls work so well only because we all know the etiquette: we know that when the phone rings we have to pick it up and say 'hello', and we know how to finish off a call by saying 'goodbye' and putting down the receiver. We know that we have to wait for the other person to stop speaking before replying (though we may say the odd 'yes', 'no' or 'uh-huh' now and again, so they know we're still there). If for some reason we can't hear what's being said, we say so, and wait for the other person to repeat it. And we speak in the same language.

In a similar way, computers can only communicate successfully with other computers over the telephone if both machines are 'speaking' in the same way, and obeying the same rules of 'conversation'. How to ensure that this happens is the subject matter of most of this chapter.

Microcomputers and modems

First things first, however. Almost by definition, teleworking involves using computers. What sort of machine is likely to be sitting on the teleworker's desk or table?

The majority of personal computers sold at present in Britain are IBM-compatible PCs, from a wide number of different manufacturers and with prices ranging from a few hundred to several thousand pounds. The cheapest PCs are generally machines using the basic 8086 or 8088 processor, and equipped with two floppy-disk drives and a monochrome monitor. IBM-compatible PCs traditionally used 5.25" floppy disks, but there has recently been a move to the larger capacity 3.5" format.

If however your computer will be your major piece of work equipment as a teleworker, it may be worth paying a little more. One sensible investment is likely to be a hard disk: a hard disk provides vastly more storage space than is possible on floppy disks, and therefore saves a great deal of disk-swapping. One step up from computers with the 8086/8088 processor are the range of 80286 machines (computers which use Intel's more powerful 80286 processor chips or equivalent). The next members of Intel's family of processors, the 386 range, are more powerful again, with 486-based machines currently top of the range and selling primarily to corporate bodies.

IBM-compatible PCs traditionally use Microsoft's MS DOS as the operating system, though Microsoft's graphics-based operating system, Windows 3.0, has proved popular recently with users with more powerful machines. Windows 3 follows the lead set by Apple Macintosh in creating a graphics-led interface between the computer and its user. Apple Mac computers, while not compatible with PC machines, have their own loyal adherents and are often the choice where more sophisticated graphics work is to be undertaken. Atari ST computers, which are also non-compatible with PCs, are also in widespread use.

The Amstrad PCW range are sold as word processors, at prices starting at about £300; they double up perfectly adequately as low-cost basic computers, however, though the technology is now several years old, and therefore in computer terms positively antique. A wide range of software is available, at very low cost.

Apart from the Amstrad PCW range which comes as a package, choosing a computer system involves selecting not simply the basic hardware but also ensuring you have an appropriate printer and screen for your requirements. A good quality monitor can help to reduce potential eye-strain; the most common display standard for monitors at present in use is known as VGA. (Various extensions of the normal VGA standard are also available.)

Computer technology changes fast, and this book in any case is not the place for a detailed look at what is available: if you are unable to find a trustworthy computer consultant or retailer locally, computer magazines available in newsagents often contain useful tips, as well as covering new product launches and technological developments. It is worth choosing carefully, however, particularly if you will need to ensure compatibility with other machines – if, for example, you are likely to exchange floppy disks with an employer or with clients.

Whatever sort of computer you have, you will need a modem before you can link it into the normal telephone network. A modem's task is to convert the stream of digital information emerging from the back of the computer into a form suitable for sending down the telephone lines, and in doing the same process in reverse for incoming signals. This process is known as modulation and demodulation; a modem is simply a modulator-demodulator.

Modems cost from about £80 upwards. A typical modem is a small, rather plain rectangular box with a row of lights at the front.

One cable from the modem goes to the serial port (socket) at the back of the computer; a second smaller wire from the modem has a telephone jack and is plugged into an ordinary BT socket. Data arrives from the computer via the serial port and cable, is duly modulated, and then sent out through the telephone wire.

Portable modems are also available, and are generally sold for use with laptop computers; they are usually about the size of a packet of butter. Alternatively, modem cards can be obtained for some computers; these are fitted directly into internal expansion slots inside the computer.

Almost any sort of microcomputer can be used with a modem. Make sure you are using the correct cable to connect your modem to the serial port (just because your cable physically fits both devices doesn't necessarily mean that the wiring inside the cable will be correct: it is best to buy the modem cable at the same time as the modem). Users of some inexpensive computers, in particular the Amstrad PCW range, will find that they also need to purchase the serial port itself, known technically as a RS-232C or V24 interface.

Modem speeds

Modems can operate at different speeds. The speed at which data is sent down the telephone line is measured in bits per second. A bit is the smallest unit of information used by a computer – it is a single binary digit, either 1 (on) or 0 (off). (Bear in mind that, using the standard computer 'alphabet' ASCII, it takes seven bits to identify an ordinary letter, number or other character.)

300 bits/sec is the slowest normal speed at which modems work, and is sometimes known as the V21 standard (the 'V' standards have been established by the international telecommunications organisation, the Comité Consultatif International Téléphonique et Télégraphique, or CCITT; unfortunately slightly different ('Bell') standards apply in north and south America).

Many modems can also send and receive data at 1200 bits/sec ('V22'), and some can also work at the even faster speed of 2400 bits/sec ('V22 bis'). Higher speeds, up to 9600 bits/sec and beyond, are also increasingly being introduced; however the problem is that the faster the transmission, the more likelihood there is that telephone line 'noise' will corrupt the data. In practice, 2400 bits/sec is likely to be the fastest you will be able to send data, and you may have to drop your modem's speed below this if the line quality is poor. However, in general the faster the modem speed the better - the less time you will be on-line, and therefore the smaller your phone bills. In particular, if you are using on-line databases which charge by access time you will want to be linked up to the remote computer for as short a time as possible.

Many cheaper modems only operate on the V21 (300 bits/sec) and V23 standards. V23 is a split speed arrangement, where data is received at 1200 bits/sec but only transmitted by your modem at 75 bits/sec. This is used, for example, for BT's Prestel viewdata service, where most of the communication is one way: the information is coming in at 1200 bits/sec from the remote computer, and it is only necessary occasionally to send short instructions back at the slower speed.

To put these speeds into perspective, it is worth bearing in mind that the fully digital Integrated Services Digital Network promises transfer speeds for data two hundred or more times faster than the basic 300 bits/sec standard. The spread of ISDN will make existing modems redundant – and indeed almost prehistoric in their technology.

Modem speeds are sometimes described in terms of the 'baud rate', so that a speed of 300 bits/sec, for example, may also be described as 300 baud rate. This is apparently a slightly incorrect usage technically speaking, although in practice the two terms are interchangeable.

If you are arranging for your computer to call up another computer, you will need to ensure that the remote computer can cope with the modem speed you have chosen. In some cases, communication will be impossible if you have picked the wrong speed: it may be a process of trial and error until you stumble on the right speed. In other cases, the remote computer may be able to sense your speed, and adjust to it accordingly.

Data bits and Parity checking

Personal computers communicate in what is called an 'asynchronous' mode: that is, discrete sets of bits are sent parcelled up together, separated by additional 'start' and 'stop' bits. (This can be compared to the words and pauses in an ordinary voice conversation.) There are two main conventions. The first is to send 7 data bits together; this corresponds with the standard ASCII alphabet range, and means that one letter or symbol would be sent at a time. The second convention is to send 8 data bits together; this allows the extended ASCII alphabet of 256 characters, commands or symbols to be transmitted.

A simple form of error-checking is generally included when 7 data bits are being sent together; this is done by adding on an extra check bit, known as the parity bit. The general principle is very basic, and relies on the fact that the sum total of all the 1s and 0s in each set of bits must be either even or odd. If 'even parity' is being followed, the extra parity bit will be set at 1 for blocks which total an odd number and at 0 for blocks which are already even, so that the eight bits together always come out as an even number. If for some reason a block arrives which isn't even, then it is clear that the block has been corrupted in transfer.

The two most common conventions for asynchronous communication are 7 bits even parity (sometimes abbreviated to '7 even') and 8 bits no parity ('8 none'). Most electronic mail services operate on a 7 even basis, while most hobbyist bulletin boards choose the 8 none convention. However, there are a number of other possibilities, and once again an element of trial and error may sometimes be necessary if you are attempting to reach an unfamiliar on-line service.

Comms software

You instruct your modem which speed and parity conventions to follow via communications software. There is a wide choice of comms software, including some good software packages available as 'shareware' (this is the computer industry's equivalent of the honesty box principle: the software is available simply for the price of a disk, but you are asked to send the software writer a payment if you find that it meets your requirements).

Most comms software programs allow you to build up your own dialling directory for the on-line services you use, so that you pre-programme in the phone number, speed and parity setting. You are also likely to be asked to define certain other things for each service. These may include:

- **'Handshaking'/Flow control**

Often when two computers are communicating one can handle data faster than the other. Flow control allows the slower machine to tell the other that it needs time to catch up. There are a number of flow control, or 'handshaking', methods; the simplest is known as XON/XOFF.

- **Echo**

In most circumstances, the text you are sending from your computer will be sent through your modem down to the distant computer and then returned by that computer to your screen: this is known as 'distant echo'. It provides a useful way of checking whether your communication is safely arriving at the other end. In some situations however it may be necessary to set your software for 'local echo' (i.e. characters are sent from your own computer to the screen).

- **File transfer protocols**

Parity checking is a very basic form of error-checking. There are a number of other much more sophisticated ways of ensuring that files are transferred safely, without errors creeping in. These are known as file transfer protocols.

One of the most widely-used protocols is called X-modem; there are a number of different refinements of this, including a protocol known as Y-modem. Another common protocol is Kermit (yes, named after the Muppets' frog).

Protocols are essential is you want to transfer non-ASCII non-text files – if for example you want to send or receive binary computer programs. For instance the network of local bulletin boards (see page 91) run by computer enthusiasts frequently have extensive databases of free 'public domain' software and of shareware programs, which you can transfer down to your own computer (this is known as 'downloading'; transferring a file from your computer to another is known as 'uploading').

If all this sounds complicated, the reality is that there is no particular reason why you have to understand the technical intricacies of computer comms before successfully putting your computer on-line. If you need further information, try the manual of your comms software package, or one of the books mentioned at the end of this chapter. If you have difficulty connecting your computer to an on-line host, try first altering the modem speed or parity setting.

Making the most of on-line time

In general, you will want to be on-line for the shortest time possible. You will normally have to pay the ordinary telephone costs of using the telephone line; but for many on-line services you will also have to pay additional, much more substantial, time-linked charges.

It is not sensible, therefore, to type in anything more than very short commands at your keyboard whilst on-line. Instead, prepare what you want to communicate beforehand, saving it on the computer as a file. Then, once you have called up the distant computer, you can simply instruct your computer (through the comms software) to send the file you specify.

Exactly the same rule applies in reverse. If you want to download a file from another computer, save it to disk on your own computer. Once you are safely off-line, you can then arrange to print out the file you have saved, or call it up on the screen. This procedure is particularly important if you intend to consult on-line commercial information databases, when access charges can be set at several pounds a minute.

Packet switching

It's quite possible to use the ordinary trunk telephone network to dial up a computer the other end of the country, or indeed the other side of the world. One disadvantage with doing this is the high telephone bills you are likely to get, especially if you begin to make many overseas calls. A second snag is that the quality of the ordinary telephone network may not be adequate over long distances to ensure that your communications arrive uncorrupted.

It is frequently better, therefore, to switch your call as quickly as possible on to a line dedicated just to transferring data. These special networks are known as packet switching systems (sometimes also called public data networks). Your call is transferred from the ordinary telephone lines to the packet switching system at a local 'node' or packet switching exchange; here the information you are sending will be amalgamated with other data being sent by other users into a number of 'packets' of data. Your particular message will be electronically tagged, so that when it reaches its destination it can be separated off from the rest of its packet, and sent on its way to the final destination. (The process of creating and dismantling the data packets is undertaken at each packet switching exchange by the Packet Assembler/Disassembler or PAD.) In practice, this process is transparent: everything takes place without the end-user being aware of what is happening.

British Telecom have the most widely used packet switching system in Britain, PSS Dialplus. (Dialplus is an improved – and more expensive – version of the BT original service, Packet SwitchStream, which is now being phased out.) There are nodes (access points) to Dialplus in over sixty towns, which means that the majority of telephone subscribers are able to make calls via Dialplus at local call charges. However, to use Dialplus you normally will need to sign up as a subscriber, and receive your own password. The fixed charge is currently £60 plus VAT a year, together with a further once-off charge of £60 plus VAT. You then pay connection charges, which work out at present at about 3p a minute.

However, a number of on-line services allow you to access them on a reverse charge basis through Dialplus, so that they pay the Dialplus charges (and normally collect them back from you in other ways). This means that you may be able to use Dialplus without taking out your own subscription. For convenience, the current phone numbers for local Dialplus nodes are given in Appendix 1.

There are several other British companies also offering packet switching services. For example, Mercury's service (Mercury 5000) is extensive, with nodes in most major cities and in less obvious centres like Truro, Newmarket and Grange-over-Sands.

INFORMATION

PSS Dialplus. Direct Response Unit, BT Managed Network Services, PO Box 1351, London NW2 7HZ. Tel: 0800 200700
Mercury 5000, Mercury Communications Ltd, Brentside Executive Centre, Great West Road, Brentford, Middx TW8 9DS. Tel: 081 914 2500

Packet switching services are also available internationally (IPSS) to many overseas countries, from Argentina to Zimbabwe. Normally, IPSS is a more advisable way of sending data than relying on direct dialling a modem abroad through the normal telephone service. BT produce an excellent free booklet with further information (see page 65).

An example: accessing Telecom Gold

It seems appropriate to conclude this chapter with a practical demonstration, by going on-line to Telecom Gold. Telecom Gold is an electronic mail and database service run by BT, which we shall be looking at again in due course. It is useful for our present purpose because it has set up a demonstration on-line database freely available to any on-line user; furthermore this can be reached either by direct dialling or via Dialplus. The actual process of obtaining access to the demonstration database is also identical to the procedure which has to be followed by Telecom Gold subscribers when using the service for real.

So the exercise which follows should give a good taste of what to expect on-line. (The procedure given is correct at the time of publication, but of course may be changed in the future.)

To dial direct, set your modem either for 7 bits even parity or 8 bits no parity; any speed up to 2400 bits/sec is acceptable. Now dial 081-203 3033. You should be greeted by a message something like this:

> Welcome to the Telecom Gold Network: For assistance type "CALL LOGIN" at the prompt "PAD>"
> This is Dial-Up, PAD 7 Line 02
> PAD>

The last line is a prompt, asking you which of the various Telecom Gold systems you want to access. The demonstration database is on system 04, so type

> PAD>CALL 04

In due course you should receive the message:

> Welcome to Telecom Gold System 04
> Please Sign On:
> >

Reply as follows (making sure you get the spacing right):

> >id GOLD-DEMO4

You will next be prompted for your password. This time simply type GOLD-DEMO4, and you should be admitted to the demonstration database. You are now free to explore the various options on offer for as long as you please. (Just remember that you will be paying for the cost of a telephone call to an 081- London number whilst you do so.) Follow the instructions and type 'LO' when you want to leave ('log off') the service.

We will now access the same demonstration database, but this time through the packet switching system PSS Dialplus. (This will have the advantage for non-Londoners of reducing the cost of the phone charges, probably to a local call rate.) First check Appendix 1 for the nearest local Dialplus node to you. Dial this number (modem settings as above).

On connection you should see a welcome screen something as follows (if the screen remains blank, try hitting the carriage return key twice, to 'wake up' the Dialplus node):

PSS Dialplus 18-Apr-1991
British Telecom

Welcome to
P S S D I A L P L U S
Datacommunications made easy
Reliable, cost-effective and error-free

(C) British Telecommunications plc 1989

If problems occur, please telephone
0800 181555, quoting the following:
Halifax   m03   MCPD3100

To access Dialplus, type your password
and press RETURN:

At this prompt, you would normally have to give your Dialplus subscriber's password. However Telecom Gold users can use Dialplus without being individual Dialplus subscribers. So simply type GOLD04 at the password prompt. You should now be taken straight to Telecom Gold system 4, where you enter the demonstration ID and password as above, and once again have the opportunity to explore the database at your leisure.

Further reading

International Data Services: A Guide for Business Personal Computer Users, (free, publ British Telecom International, Holborn Centre, 120 Holborn, London EC1N 2TE. Tel: 0800 272172).

Communications for Progress, A Guide to International e-mail, Graham Lane (£6.99, publ CIIR). (This is primarily written for voluntary third world organisations but offers a good general introduction to comms issues.)

New Hacker's Handbook, 4th ed revised Steve Gold, (publ Century). (Withdrawn by the publishers after anti-hacking legislation became law. However, this is more of an enthusiastic romp through the world of computer comms than a manual for those with criminal intent. Good practical information for all on-line users.)

6
WHAT'S AVAILABLE ON-LINE?:
1 INFORMATION DATABASES

'If it's a question which has an answer, the answer will be available on-line,' a friend confidently asserted to me. He may have been exaggerating a little, but in essence he was probably right: the chances are that, whatever information you may need, it is stored in a public database on a computer somewhere in the world, ready for you to access. Put your microcomputer on-line, get your modem to dial the right number, and the information can be downloaded straight into your own computer.

The development of on-line databases is potentially of immense importance to teleworkers. Outside, the local mobile library may push its way through the hills to reach your village only once every few weeks; inside, however, you have the equivalent of a comprehensive academic and commercial library ready and waiting at your computer workstation. It is as though your chair at home doubles up as a seat permanently available for you in the British Library reading room.

Nevertheless, the existence of these on-line database services is somthing of a well-kept secret. Few people outside the world of professional librarians and information workers have yet begun to explore what is available on-line; and those that have have sometimes been very put off by what they've encountered.

This is perhaps because, ironically, the one question for which the answer may not be available on-line is the basic one: how do you get started? Given the structure of the on-line database industry, it can be difficult to know where to turn for the help you need, and very difficult to know which are the best ways to save money.

For the uninitiated, in fact, the experience of going on-line can turn into something of a nightmare: rather as though you suddenly were to find yourself in an extensive reference library, with not a librarian in sight, no sign of any kind of catalogue, and all the book titles mysteriously erased from their spines, but where you knew you were being charged £2 for every minute you remained there. (To complete the analogy, you might only later find out that you could have paid less if you'd entered the library through a back-door, or via a trapdoor from the floor above.)

Perhaps this is a little unfair. However, one difficulty with the on-line database industry is that the same databases can often be reached in several different ways, and that the charges will vary depending on which route you have chosen. The task therefore is not only to identify which database will have the information you require, but to decide in addition how you intend to access it.

It is estimated that there are now something in the region of 5,000 publicly available on-line databases worldwide, of which perhaps 500 are British-based. Some of these are available free of charge – one example is the British Electronic Yellow Pages database (EYP), which we shall look at in a moment. In most cases, however, you will have to pay to conduct a search. The charges imposed may seem very steep – several pounds a minute is not necessarily untypical, for example. However, provided you know what you are doing, it is generally possible to extract the information you need very quickly, so that your total time on-line is limited. It may make commercial sense to spend, say, £20 on a quick on-line search rather than spend half a day trying to find the same information from more conventional sources. The knack is, as we saw in the last chapter, to use the highest modem speed you can and to save the information to a computer file: don't try to read it until you are safely off-line.

The on-line database industry really began at the start of the 'Seventies, but has grown fast; in Britain, the market is increasing by about 20%-25% a year, according to one recent market research survey. At the moment, the vast majority of searches are undertaken by librarians or professional information workers, acting as intermediaries; however, there is a welcome move by some database companies to encourage more 'end-users' to undertake their own searches. Until recently, it has generally been necessary to learn specific command languages in order to search particular databases successfully; however, there are already moves to introduce more user-friendly 'front-ends', to remove some of the technical problems involved in the actual searching.

Originally, most on-line databases were bibliographical: typically, for example, abstracts of scientific or academic journal articles. Bibliographical databases are still present in considerable numbers (one example is the US database ABI/Inform, which we look at later); however, there has recently been a move towards full-text databases, where newspaper or magazine articles are available in full (Profile is the example we shall consider.) Finally, there are also a considerable number of numeric or combined text/numeric databases, such as those carrying statistical information.

Some databases will be of general interest; others will appeal only to a specialist audience. COFFEELINE is a database containing literature about coffee production, for example; PESTDOC has information about agricultural pests; BRIX is produced by the Building Research Establishment; JUSTIS is a legal database... and so on.

In some cases, databases may be marketed by the company which has compiled the information. More often, however, databases are made available through 'host' services, electronic retailers who may have anything from a handful to several hundred databases held on their own computers (there are perhaps 600-700 hosts worldwide). The on-line database industry is an international one, and many British people choose to undertake searches using one of the large overseas host services, such as DIALOG in California and Data-Star in Switzerland.

A further complication is the use of 'gateways', electronic links between computers which enable some databases to be accessed from other services.

Details about the main host services are given later in this chapter; first however we shall look at a small selection of databases, to give some sort of idea of the range of information available.

Example: Phone Base

We shall begin by looking at a new database which may give many people their first taste of on-line searching.

When British Telecom introduced charges for their directory enquiry service in 1991, they also made their subscriber database publicly available, marketing it under the name Phone Base. (Rather embarrassingly they forgot to take out all the ex-directory information when they first made it public, but that's another story.)

In general, Phone Base is likely to cost you less than calling the normal directory enquiry service, provided you already have a computer and modem. You find the number you want by entering the surname or business name and the town (it is advisable not to enter too much detail).

The Phone Base computer is in fact based in Sheffield, but all calls to it are charged at BT's b1 rate (the reduced long distance rate) – even in fact if you are calling from Sheffield. This works out at present at 6p-13p a minute, depending on time of access. At the moment, there are no other charges involved; however, and rather unhelpfully, BT only make the service available to those who have registered as subscribers, and have been issued with an ID and password. BT say that this is only as a security measure, and that in due course they hope to move to open access.

Access to Phone Base is also available via a gateway from Prestel (see page 81); BT say that access via the Dialplus packet switching service will also be introduced in the future.

INFORMATION

For more details about Phone Base, telephone, Tel: 0800 800802/800899
Helpdesk. Tel: 0800 919199
On-line (via modem): 0910 210910 (1200/75 speeds only; 8 none)
You can also arrange to see Phone Base demonstrated for you in a number of BT centres including London, Manchester, Leeds, Bristol, Birmingham and Bracknell.

Example: Electronic Yellow Pages (EYP)

The other major BT on-line directory demands no advance registration from its users. In fact, as the service is designed to attract advertising, users are able to dial in at local call rates. Like the Yellow Pages themselves, EYP offers a listing of commercial and business phone numbers: just the place to search for florists in Fowey or auctioneers in Auchtermuchty.

Like Phone Base, EYP can be a little difficult for first-time users (there are a number of irritating search features, for example), although it's worth persevering. Apart from the direct dial number, it is also possible to get to EYP via packet-switching (though this will cost you more), or via a Prestel gateway.

INFORMATION

Helpdesk. Tel: 0734 506506
On-line (via modem): 0345 444444 (any modem speeds up to 2400 bits/sec)

Example: Profile

Profile began life modestly enough almost ten years ago, when (under the name World Reporter) it was created as a way of making transcripts of BBC news broadcasts available to a wider audience. Much has changed since then, and Profile – now part of the *Financial Times* group – has become a valuable research tool for many different situations.

Profile offers the full text of a wide range of British and overseas newspapers and magazines. Publications available via Profile include all the quality British dailies (the *Financial Times, The Times, The Guardian, The Daily Telegraph* and *The Independent*) plus several Sunday papers. Many magazines are also included, including *New Scientist, Marketing, Campaign* and the *Economist*. There are international sources of news, including the *Washington Post, TASS* and the *Wall Street Journal*. There are also specialist publications carried, including market research and stockbroker reports.

Of course, all this doesn't guarantee that Profile is necessarily of any more use than a pile of yellowing newspapers would be. Fortunately, however, it's relatively easy to find the exact articles you want. To use Profile, you first identify the publication, or groups of publications, you want to search. You might enter the command SELECT GDN, for example, to choose the *Guardian* database.

Next you enter, using the 'GET' command, the subject(s) or name(s) you are interested in researching: let's say GET TELEWORKING.

Profile will quickly identify every article from *The Guardian* which contains this term, and tell you how many 'hits' it has made. The headlines of each article can be displayed (HEADLINE ALL), you can choose to read the full text of each article (TEXT ALL), or perhaps ask merely to see the paragraphs in which the selected word appeared (CONTEXT ALL). Or you can choose to view only selected articles.

For the record, I can report that *The Guardian* has indeed taken an interest in teleworking, as indeed have the other British papers – a Profile search of the national press turned up over 50 'hits' over a three year period.

Profile can be used, as in this case, to obtain background information of a subject, but can also be used to find out more about individuals or about companies. Or you can treat it as a cuttings service, to identify occasions when your own company or name has appeared in print.

It is possible to subscribe to Profile direct: the subscription is currently a one-off £250 plus VAT, which includes two user manuals, two free training courses, and free on-line time in the first month. Searches currently cost 75p a minute, plus a lineage rate (normally 3p a line) for each line retrieved. (All prices exclude VAT.) However, Profile is also widely available through many other hosts on a simple time charge basis – Telecom Gold for example currently levy an access charge of £2.20 per minute plus VAT. For the occasional Profile user, it may be better to reach the database through a host service rather than subscribing direct.

INFORMATION

FT Profile, PO Box 12, Sunbury-on-Thames, Middx TW16 7UD.
Helpline. Tel: 0932 787231
On-line (via modem): 0932 781111 (300 or 2400 bits/sec); 781144 (1200 bits/sec); 785688 (1200/75 bits/sec)
Profile produce a free quarterly newsletter, *Offline*, available on request

Profile competes with two other on-line services offering access to the full text of newspaper and magazine articles:

INFORMATION

Reuters Textline. Reuters Ltd, 85 Fleet Street, London EC4P 4AJ.
Tel: 071 250 1122
LEXIS-NEXIS. Mead Data Central International, International House,
1 St Katherine's Way, London E1 9UN. Tel: 071 488 9187

Example: ICC UK companies database

The information which by law all British limited companies have to register at Companies House provides the raw material which several database companies use for on-line services. ICC's UK Companies database is typical. ICC say that they carry at least basic information about 2 million or so limited companies – all the live companies (c 1.2m) currently trading, plus others which have been dissolved in recent years.

A search of the ICC UK companies' database will allow you to turn up the correct company name, date of incorporation and registered office. For about three-quarters of a million companies, a little financial information is also provided: typically the company's turnover figure or total net assets. However, the records of about 180,000 companies have substantially more detail, including profit and loss account and balance sheet reports and growth rate statistics. ICC also offer their assessment of these companies' credit-worthiness.

ICC's UK Companies database is available directly or through many host services. However, it is a little invidious to mention ICC and not also point out that there are several other competing firms offering company information database services. Details follow.

INFORMATION

ICC Information Services, Field House, 72 Oldfield Rd, Hampton,
Tel: 081 783 1122

Infocheck, 28 Scrutton Street, London EC2A 4RQ Tel: 071 377 8872
Jordan and Sons, 47 Brunswick Place, London N1 6EE Tel: 071 253 3030
Kompass On-line, Windsor Court, East Grinstead House, East Grinstead, West Sussex, RH19 1XA Tel: 0342 326972

Example: ABI/Inform

By contrast with our previous examples, this is a bibliographical database, produced in the USA. ABI/Inform offers abstracts of articles in about 800 periodicals, primarily in the areas of business and management. Some non-English language publications are also monitored.

ABI/Inform dates back to August 1971, and claims now to have something in the region of half a million records in the database. Despite its transatlantic bias, ABI/Inform is widely used in Britain, and an ABI/Inform search can be an effective way of identifying current thinking or academic research in areas of interest. Searching is by subject or category code.

For the record, a search undertaken during the writing of this book turned up references to over 200 journal articles referring to teleworking written since the mid-1980s, from publications as various as *Telephony, Equal Opportunities International* and *California Management Review*.

ABI/Inform is reached via one of the major database hosts – and it is the services these hosts offer that we shall now turn to consider.

Database hosts

The database hosts are the supermarkets of the on-line world, gathering together under one electronic roof a wide range of databases from different producers.

As with grocery shopping, different hosts are likely to be offering many of the same products (DIALOG, Data-Star, Orbit and several other hosts all offer ABI/Inform, for example). However there are some databases (generally more specialist ones) which are only carried by one particular host.

Although on-line search charges may vary – perhaps substantially – depending on which host you choose to use, in practice most people tend to stick with one or two host services. This is partly because it takes time to become familiar with the particular search commands and techniques you need to use with each host. It is also because it is simpler only to have to pay one or two accounts each month.

DIALOG has become the market leader in Britain, despite the fact that it is a Californian-based service and sends in its bill in dollars. This is primarily because of the large number of databases to which DIALOG provides access – about 350 in all. Database searching has recently become a little easier for inexperienced users with the introduction of a menu-led service as an alternative to DIALOG's traditional command language; currently about two-thirds of the databases can be accessed through the menu service.

DIALOG has a UK office and offers regular training courses in this country, including initial free demonstration sessions each month in London. On-line access to California is via DIALOG's own data communications network DIALNET, which can be reached either by direct dialling an 071-number or via your local PSS Dialplus node (this is available whether or not you subscribe directly to Dialplus). The connection charge is at present $10 an hour.

Apart from the cost of connection, DIALOG's charging structure is based on connect time, which varies between databases from $15 to $300 per hour and averages about $70 per hour. There is also an annual fixed fee of $35.

DIALOG also has a cheaper after-hours service, the Knowledge Index, which has been set up primarily for home computer users, and is available only in the evenings and early hours. About 90 DIALOG databases are available through the Knowledge Index, at a standard access charge of $24 an hour (including, in this instance, the DIALNET connection). A separate $35 annual fee applies to users of the Knowledge Index

INFORMATION

Dialog, PO Box 188, Oxford OX1 5AX. Tel: 0865 730275

By contrast to DIALOG, Data-Star is a European-based host: it is in fact located in Switzerland, and linked to Radio Suisse. Data-Star provides access to about 150 databases, primarily in the fields of business and finance, medicine and health care, biotechnology, chemistry and technology. Although offering a smaller choice than DIALOG, Data-Star is more closely tailored to European users' needs; it may also be cheaper to use than DIALOG.

As with DIALOG, access to Data-Star can be obtained by dialling your local PSS Dialplus node. On-line charges are a combination of time charges (ranging from about £15-£120 per hour), plus document charges for files displayed or saved to disk (these vary from a few pence upwards). There are discounts for customers prepared to commit themselves in advance to a certain level of usage; there is no annual fixed fee.

Like DIALOG, Data-Star has recently introduced a menu-led service for less experienced users. Data-Star also provide free on-line training files, and regular training seminars in London and Liverpool.

INFORMATION

Data-Star, Plaza Suite, 114 Jermyn Street, London SW1Y 6HJ. Tel: 071 930 5503

Another European host is ESA-IRS, an offshoot of the European Space Agency project. ESA-IRS have approximately 100 databases available, in the areas of science and technology, and business. Access is available again through PSS Dialplus, with an ESA-IRS supplied password.

Charging is primarily on a document retrieval basis – so that ESA-IRS argue that searchers can spend longer on-line finding exactly the files they need, before incurring significant charges. The British end of the ESA-IRS operation (which has its head office in Italy) is now run by an offshoot of the British Library.

INFORMATION

ESA-IRS, IRS/DIALTECH, Science Reference Information Service, 25 Southampton Buildings, Chancery Lane, London WC2 1AW. Tel: 071 323 7951/7946

Robert Maxwell's empire extends to the on-line database world. Maxwell Online includes two host services, BRS and Orbit. BRS claims to specialise in databases concerned with medicine, pharmacology, life sciences, psychology, humanities, education and business. Orbit includes over 100 databases specialising in chemistry, energy issues, engineering, health & safety, metarials science and patents.

INFORMATION

Maxwell Online, Achilles House, Western Avenue, London W3 0UA. Tel: 0800 289512; or 081 992 3456

Several of these hosts run electronic mail services, as offshoots of their main operation. Conversely, it is also possible to access a number of databases from what are primarily electronic mail services. These include, as we have seen, Telecom Gold. Another e-mail service, Poptel/GeoNet see page 89 provides access to various databases via a facility known as Intelligent Information (ii). ii is a 'front-end' menu-driven service, which automatically undertakes the actual database searching for you.

INFORMATION

Poptel/GeoNet, 25 Downham Rd, London N1 5AA. Tel: 071 249 2948

Other on-line hosts

It may also be useful to mention two other specialist hosts. The British Library operates two services; Blaise-Line offers access to the BL's own catalogues, as well as to Whitaker's British Books in Print and the HMSO catalogue. Blaise-Link is a special link to with the US National Library of Medicine, providing a tie-up with the US MEDLINE database.

INFORMATION

BLAISE Information Services, The British Library, Boston Spa, Wetherby, West Yorkshire LS23 7BQ Tel: 0937 546585

The European Community's on-line service, ECHO, is a non-commercial host set up to make the developments within the Community, and the decisions taken by the European Commission, more widely available. Most of the ECHO databases can be accessed without charge.

INFORMATION

European Commission Host Organisation, B.P. 2373, L-1023 Luxembourg G.D. Tel: (+352) 488041

Help and information

If you're approaching on-line database searching for the first time, it's sensible to make use of other people's experiences. A good place to go for informal advice can be your nearest large local reference library; most larger libraries are likely to have at least one member of staff with on-line search experience who may be happy to pass on suggestions and advice.

The UK On-Line User Group (UKOLUG) is a network of individuals, primarily librarians and information professionals, interested in on-line searching. UKOLUG produces an informative bi-monthly newsletter, and also arranges conferences and seminars. In some parts of the country, there are also local on-line users' groups, affiliated to UKOLUG.

UKOLUG is a sub-group of the Institute of Information Scientists, and IIS members are able to join for a reduced subscription. Non-members are invited to join at a current subscription of £12.

INFORMATION

UKOLUG, c/o Institute of Information Scientists, 44-45 Museum St, London WC1A 1LY. Tel: 071 831 8003/8633

The on-line industry's major annual showcase is the Online Information conference and exhibition, held normally every December in Olympia, London. The conference is organised by Learned Information (Europe) Ltd, who also produce a monthly newspaper,

Information World Review with news of on-line developments, and various other publications.

INFORMATION

Learned Information Ltd, Woodside, Hinksey Hill, Oxford OX1 5AU.
Tel: 0865-730275

7
WHAT'S AVAILABLE ON-LINE?:
2 VIDEOTEX

Like the on-line commercial databases we looked at in the last chapter, 'videotex' services such as BT's Prestel also offer access to information. Videotex has its own history and its own particular niche in the market, however, and is worth considering separately.

Videotex has established a significant role in several industries: it is widely used in the insurance world, for example, allowing High Street brokers to receive up-to-date information on policy details and prices from a range of different insurance companies. It has become an almost essential feature of the travel agency business, where it is used for booking customers' holidays, obtaining information and ordering new stocks of brochures. Stockbrokers, educational institutions, local authorities and many others also have their own specialist uses for the technology.

Videotex has not broken through into the mass market in Britain in the way that it has in France, however. The French télétel service got off to a flying start when France Telecom gave away hundreds of thousands of free 'Minitel' terminals in the early 1980s, as an on-line substitute for the traditional telephone directory service. All sorts of things are now marketed through Minitel (including the rather insalubrious type of lonely hearts chatline which in Britain has found a home on BT's 0898 numbers), and it is estimated that there are now over five million Minitel terminals.

By contrast, BT's equivalent service Prestel has been much slower to get established. Nevertheless, videotex services like Prestel may still have something to offer home-based teleworkers.

It's perhaps best to start with some definitions. The rather ugly term 'videotex' encompasses both 'teletext' services (such as the BBC's Ceefax and the ITV companies' Oracle) where data is communicated using broadcasting signals, and 'viewdata' services, where – as in the case of Prestel – it is the telephone wire which acts as the delivery method.

Both technologies developed in the early 1970s. The Ceefax and Oracle teletext services make use of the fact that not all of the 625 lines that make up an ordinary television picture are used for the TV signal; a few lines (normally out of sight at the edge of the TV screen) can therefore be pressed into use to carry other information. Ceefax and Oracle pages are encoded and sent out with normal TV signals, to be decoded by the special teletext receivers supplied in some TV sets. As well as the normal Ceefax/Oracle public service, the same system is used to carry private information for some corporate clients, who have their own specially configured terminals. Ceefax and Oracle offer what is primarily a one-way news and leisure-orientated service (though cable TV promises new opportunities).

By contrast, videotex services like Prestel which use the telephone lines for data communications can be interactive, so that the user is able to send information back to the host computer. Prestel was originally designed to work with a special dedicated terminal and ordinary TV; however the service was given a considerable boost by the development of microcomputers, and most Prestel users now access the service using a computer keyboard and modem. However, it is still necessary to ensure that your communications software is set up for the necessary 'viewdata' emulation – in other words, so that your computer imitates the way a Prestel terminal works. As another relic of the past, Prestel is accessed at the split rate speed of 1200/75 bits per second – in other words, data is sent from the host computer at the full 1200 bits/sec, but can only be sent back at the slow speed of 75 bits/sec.

An introduction to Prestel

Unless your work means that you make use of commercial videotex services supplied by other carriers, it is Prestel which is likely to be of most interest to you. Prestel operates on a frame-by-frame basis (in contrast to the continuous text basis of the on-line database services considered in the last chapter). Each frame (or 'page') has its own number, identified by an initial asterisk and final hash symbol: so that for example Prestel page *199# is the main A-

Z index. If you know the page you require, you can jump straight there; otherwise you follow a chain of menus, page by page, until finally – with luck – you find the information you require. There are in the region of a quarter of a million separate frames.

This trunk and branch approach to its database is both Prestel's strength and weakness. On the one hand, it is relatively easy for an inexperienced user to use the menu systems to negotiate their way around the Prestel maze, provided they have the time and patience. However, the interminable series of menus, sub-menus and sub-sub-menus can be extremely tedious if you are used to more sophisticated on-line services.

Prestel, like Telecom Gold, is operated by a subsidiary of British Telecom and is described by them as an electronic publishing medium. Some of the pages of information on Prestel have been supplied by BT itself, but much of the information on Prestel has been put up by other organisations and businesses, either as a public service or (more usually) as a marketing or an income-generating undertaking. These bodies are known as 'information providers' or IPs. They include familiar names such as British Rail, British Airways, the AA and the Meteorological Office, as well as much smaller concerns. Some IPs are in business merely to sell space on Prestel on to other firms.

Because of this, there is no guarantee that the information you may require will necessarily have been made available on Prestel; unlike a good public library, for example, Prestel does not attempt to be comprehensive.

Most pages of Prestel are available on free access. However some carry a premium charge: anything from a few pence to several pounds per frame. For example, many of the leisure pages on Prestel tempt you into answering quizzes, looking at your horoscope or checking out the latest news or gossip – at a cost. 'Harder' information (such as the Meteorological Office's detailed forecasts or the AA and RAC roadwatch information) is also available only at extra cost.

Some areas of Prestel are only available on restricted access; these are known as 'closed user groups' (CUGs). One such facility is the BT Travel Service for ABTA travel agents; another is the BT Insurance

Services for brokers. One of the largest of the CUGs is another BT-owned concern, Micronet, which has been established as an on-line club for home microcomputer users. The Prestel network is also used as a private videotex transmission service for corporate clients, where obviously the information transmitted is not available for general users.

Finally, electronic links ('gateways') from the Prestel computers have been set up to other mainframe computers, so that it is possible to hop out of Prestel temporarily. There are gateways, for example, to British Rail's computer, to BT's on-line directories, as well as to financial databases such as Infocheck and Citiservice.

Details of some of the services available through Prestel are given below.

Government information

The government has made significant use of Prestel, and has over 10,000 pages of information available on the system, most of them free of additional charges. This includes details of the names of government ministers and of MPs, and a full list of government departments. There is information on the week's business in Parliament, government publications and official statistics, including the Census results. Other departments and governmental bodies contributing useful information include the Department of Trade and Industry, the Health & Safety Executive and the Department of Education and Science. There is even a list of unclaimed premium bond prizes!

The Central Office of Information publish a helpful directory of these services on Prestel, which can be ordered free of charge from Prestel page *500151#.

INFORMATION

Other useful pages include:
Page *5001# Guide to government services on Prestel
Page *500110# Alphabetical index of all government departments
Page *500024# Names of MPs, with constituencies

Page *500135# Ministers by department
Page *204# Front page for Dept of Trade and Industry

The central register maintained by the Securities and Investments Board (SIB) of all firms authorised to carry out financial business under the Financial Services Act can be reached via a gateway from Prestel (page *301#), though premium prices apply. (For enquiries about individual companies, it is cheaper to phone SIB direct, on 071-929 3652.)

BT on-line directories

Both Phone Base and Electronic Yellow Pages (see above, pages 69 and 70) are available free via gateways from Prestel. Phone Base can be used by Prestel subscribers without the need to register separately. Both these directory services can be reached – appropriately enough – via page *192#.

Travel

Because of the importance which videotex plays in the travel business, a wide range of travel companies – small as well as large – use Prestel. Times and prices of air-flights can be found for many carriers. Tickets can be ordered on-line, and brochures requested. British Rail has extensive information available – it must just be BR's luck that once when I tried to access their database I was told that their Prestel service was suspended 'due to equipment problems'! As already mentioned, the motoring organisations also use Prestel to provide information for motorists.

Home banking and shopping

The Bank of Scotland's long established home banking service operates via a Prestel gateway (page *3951#). This is known as HOBS (Home and Office Banking Service); it offers on-line bank statements, cash transfers between accounts, bill paying and certain other banking services.

The Clydesdale Bank also operate a home banking service via a videotex link; in their case, however, they have chosen a rival carrier to Prestel, Fastrak (more frequently used in the travel trade).

A number of mail-order catalogue companies, and some smaller operators, use Prestel for 'teleshopping'; orders can be placed and paid for (normally by giving credit card details) on-line. *Which?* magazine investigated teleshopping arrangements using both Prestel and other videotex services in March 1991, and concluded that, 'it does seem that teleshopping hasn't taken off as quickly as some experts thought it would, although as developments continue, it's possible that by the end of the decade more of us will be doing at least some of our shopping using a teleshopping scheme'. It may be one alternative for teleworkers who have opted for the remote lifestyle.

Communications

Apart from its use as an information source, Prestel also provides a communications link between Prestel users via an electronic mailbox service. There is also a facility for sending and receiving telex messages via this service.

Prestel charges and access arrangements

The ordinary Prestel subscription is currently £20 per quarter, with a peak-time (Monday-Saturday 8am-6pm) connect charge of 8p per minute; off-peak the rate is 3p a minute. (All prices exclude VAT.)

Users who choose to subscribe also to BT's Micronet microcomputer on-line club pay an inclusive total of £30 plus VAT per quarter, but have free off-peak access to Prestel.

BT have set up a Prestel demonstration database which can be reached free of charge, either by dialling the 071 number below, or through a local node (access point). (Contact the Prestel helpdesk for details of your nearest node.) To gain access once your call has reached the host computer, enter the digit 4 ten times when prompted for your customer identification (i.e., '4444444444'), and then a further four times when prompted for your ID ('4444'). To exit Prestel at any time, enter the code *90#.

INFORMATION

More details about Prestel: Tel: 0800 200700
Prestel Helpdesk: Tel: 0442 237237
Demonstration: On-line (via modem): 071 618 1111 (1200/75 bits/sec; 7 even).

Télétel

The French videotex service, normally reached through dedicated Minitel terminals, operates to a different technical standard to Prestel. For intrepid Britons who want a taste of the French on-line life, a London company supply the necessary software or terminal, together with a gateway into Minitel. Run a home banking account with the *Crédit Commercial de France*, check Paris-Lyon train times with SNCF, consult one of the databases of French businesses (or just practice your French).

INFORMATION

Aldoda International Ltd, 27 Elizabeth Mews, London NW3 4UH.
Tel: 071 586 5686

8
WHAT'S AVAILABLE ON-LINE?:
3 COMMUNICATIONS

A few years ago, some advocates of computer communications would shake their heads sadly when contemplating the traditional postal service: it was, they said, a 'snail-mail' service, doomed to be overtaken by the quick and efficient alternative of transferring messages via electronic mail (e-mail).

Their prediction was premature, if not completely wrong. The post is still regularly pushed through my letter-box once or twice a day, and a pile of letters lands on the floor by the front door. By contrast, my electronic mailbox frequently remains empty from one day to the next. If a revolution in communication is supposed to be taking place, rather a large number of people have yet to be told about it.

Nevertheless, electronic means of communication are potentially of great value, especially for those of us who have chosen to telework. As we shall see, facilities such as e-mail can usefully complement other more traditional forms of communication. The problem, as with on-line information databases, is that it is not necessarily very easy to find out what is available.

Direct computer-to-computer links

Computers tend not to be very good at talking to each other. There are too many different types of machine, too many incompatible operating systems and software programs to assume that files produced one on machine can be transferred easily to another.

Nevertheless, direct computer-to-computer connection is quite feasible, even for the non-specialist, provided you have a little patience. The two machines can be in the same room, joined together by cable; but they can also be hundreds or thousands of miles apart, linked via the telephone network. (In the latter case, both computers will of course need modems, to handle the flow of data through the telephone system.)

As we saw in chapter 5, successful computer communication depends on both machines operating to the same data transfer conventions, as set up through the communications software. Obviously if a computer set up to receive data is expecting it to be sent at 1200 bits/sec on an 8 bit/no parity basis, it is likely to be unable to make sense of data which comes through at 300 bits/sec in a 7 bit/even parity form. If you are transferring non-ASCII files, such a binary programs, both machines will need to be following the same file transfer protocol (see page 60). Be warned that protocols with familiar names such as X-modem, Y-modem and Kermit have been adapted and amended by software programmers over the years, so that there is no absolute guarantee that two different comms software packages offering apparently identical protocols will in reality be able to transfer data safely between machines.

For direct computer-to-computer communication to work, therefore – particularly at a distance – a fair degree of prior co-ordination is normally necessary. It may be essential for both machines to be attended while the data transfer is taking place.

Electronic mail

Electronic mail services introduce an intermediary – the e-mail host computer – to this process of information transfer between computer users.

The basic principle is simple: each e-mail subscriber is allocated a private 'space' on the host computer, known as a mailbox, into which other subscribers can deposit messages or information. The subscriber can then go on-line at any time to read these messages, or if necessary to download them into their own computer for further perusal.

British Telecom have used the analogy of a hotel pigeon-hole arrangement when publicising their own e-mail service: 'Think of Telecom Gold computers as the bank of pigeon-holes and of your mailbox as one pigeon hole,' they say. 'You don't have to be in the hotel to receive messages, and you can phone the hotel to leave messages for other people. When you come to the reception desk, you can enquire whether there are any messages waiting for you.'

If you are working at a remote location, there are obvious advantages to the e-mail system. For example, you could prepare a business report on your home computer and forward it to a colleague via their mailbox. They could then down-load it into their own computer, make any additions or corrections necessary, and then return it back to your computer – the whole process taking place without the need for sending hard-copy through the post, or retyping the document.

E-mail can also provide an electronic equivalent of the office memo, with the advantage that the same message can be sent automatically to several different mailboxes as easily as to just one subscriber. This means, for example, that the minutes of a meeting could be dispatched effortlessly to all members of the committee in one go, provided of course they all have mailboxes on the same system.

There are a considerable number of competing electronic mail services available, offering different levels of sophistication. BT's Telecom Gold is currently the market leader in Britain (details of the Telecom Gold demonstration database were given in chapter 5). Individual users are at present charged an initial registration fee of £40, with a monthly charge thereafter of £5 per mailbox. There are further charges for using the service: the main item is the connection fee (2p-6.5p a minute). However there are additional costs incurred when you send or read mail, or when you store files on the host computer (leaving your e-mail messages unread for more than a short time, in fact, can quickly turn into an expensive activity). Telecom Gold also charge for specific other facilities, such as database searching. (All figures quoted exclude VAT.)

INFORMATION

Telecom Gold enquiries – Tel: 0800 200700

One of the largest e-mail services in Europe is GeoNet. In Britain, there are two linked GeoNet e-mail services (Poptel/GeoNet and the Manchester Host); these are primarily used by non-commercial organisations and individuals. (Addresses are given later in this chapter.)

The main limitation of electronic mail in Britain at present is the lack of immediate compatibility between different e-mail services. It is rather as though there were half a dozen or more rival Royal Mail postal services, with the public restricted to sending letters only to people who happen to be with the same company. Admittedly, there are obscure gateways between different e-mail services (I recently sent an e-mail message to a friend a few miles away on a different e-mail system; in order to get through, my message had to be routed via a computer in California.)

An easier way to communicate with other e-mail systems may be to use The Direct Connection, an electronic clearing-house service who provide gateways between almost all e-mail providers worldwide. They currently charge £10 + VAT a month for this service.

INFORMATION

The Direct Connection enquiries – Tel: 081 853 2283
Information also available on-line (via modem): 081 853 3965
(speeds from 300-2400 bits/sec; type 'demo' to log in)

(It is likely that the problem of e-mail incompatibility will gradually disappear. The CCITT have established an international standard, known as X400, which is in the process of being adopted worldwide. In time, subscribers to most major e-mail services will have the opportunity of sending messages to users of other systems.)

It can be hard to get into the habit of checking your mailbox regularly for messages, particularly if your use of e-mail is light. Unfortunately, as we have seen, it can be expensive to leave messages stored unread for any length of time. Telecom Gold offer an alert scheme, whereby e-mail subscribers can be informed through a BT pager when messages arrive in their mailbox.

Telecom Gold, and most other e-mail services, also allow subscribers the opportunity to send e-mail messages direct to any fax or telex machine worldwide. This is likely to be more expensive and slower than using your own fax or telex machine – though in the case of fax, the quality of the received document will be better. Conversely, you can receive telex messages in your mailbox; e-mail therefore provides a cheap way into the telex system. Incoming faxes, as yet, cannot be received in mailboxes.

Bulletin boards

What we in Britain normally refer to as notice boards are described by Americans as 'bulletin boards'. Since in the computer industry American terminology tends to take precedence, it is not surprising that it is the latter term which is used on both sides of the Atlantic to describe their electronic counterpart.

On-line bulletin boards provide open space for messages of all kinds to be posted, to be read and discussed by other on-line users. For many people, bulletin boards are a hobby: many simple bulletin boards are run from home by computer enthusiasts who arrange for their microcomputer to be set up as the 'host' machine, linked into the telephone network; they then publicise the number and sit back waiting for other people to make contact.

Corresponding with other computer users via a bulletin board can be a useful way of improving your technical knowledge of computers – or, especially, of comms – since other bulletin board users will generally be happy to see if they can help solve your problems. But primarily amateur bulletin boards are run just for the fun of it. Some people will enjoy the activity of contributing to the on-line discussions and debates, and of exchanging free software programs; others may consider it a rather unsatisfactory sort of social life.

Hobbyist bulletin boards tend to come and go; their telephone numbers are sometimes published in the leisure-orientated computer magazines. Shareware distributors (who advertise widely in the computer press) are also likely to know what numbers to dial, since many public domain and shareware programs are available from local bulletin boards. In any case, once you have safely found one bulletin board you are likely to be able to ask on-line for other telephone numbers to try.

On-line conferences

Home-based bulletin boards may provide relaxation for hard-pressed teleworkers, but are not likely to be of much use for work purposes. However, the same basic bulletin board principles can also be used in other ways. Inconsequential bulletin board chatting can shade imperceptibly into on-line conferencing – a much grander concept, where as the name implies the participants are likely to be taking their contributions a lot more seriously.

One up from the basic bulletin boards are the informal on-line conferences, run on a number of e-mail and similar systems. Some conferences are open to all comers; in other cases, you will need to register first with the conference co-ordinator before being admitted. Yet other conferences may be operating on a strict closed user group basis – open perhaps only to employees of one company or members of the same organisation.

One on-line bulletin board/conferencing service is CIX (pronounced 'kicks'). This is run commercially, with a £15 + VAT initial registration fee and a subsequent minimum monthly charge of £6.25 + VAT (further charges depend on usage). At the time of writing, a conference has been established on CIX for home-based workers, especially teleworkers, by the magazine Live Wire.

INFORMATION

CIX Ltd, Suite 2, The Sanctuary, Oakhill Grove, Surbiton, Surrey KT6 6DU.
Tel: 081 390 8446
More information on-line (via modem): 081 390 1244 or 081 399 5252
(speeds up to 2400 bits/sec; 8 none); 081 390 9787 (9600 bits/sec)

There are a number of specialist on-line conferencing services. Rurtel, for example, is based in northern Scotland and draws most – though not all – of its participating members from the Highlands and Islands area. The service was set up in 1986 by the Arkleton Trust, an educational body concerned with rural development and education, as a way of encouraging communication in an area where geographical distances between communities can be substantial. Rurtel offers system commands in either English or Gaelic, and has a number of Gaelic language conferences. A similar pilot project Gaeltel operates in Co Galway, Ireland.

A more recent initiative is that taken by Manchester City Council. The 'Manchester Host' service, launched in Spring 1991, has been set up with financial support from the local authority to provide on-line services both for commercial companies and for community organisations and local people in the Manchester area – though already a number of subscribers from other parts of the country have joined as well. In addition to on-line conferencing, the Manchester Host provides offers an electronic mail service and access to commercial databases via Intelligent Information (ii).

As mentioned above, the Manchester Host is linked to the Poptel/ GeoNet service, which itself operates a series of conferences used by many charitable and community organisations. Poptel/GeoNet's London address is also the home of GreenNet, an environmental e-mail and conferencing system.

INFORMATION

Rurtel, The Arkleton Trust, Nethy Bridge, Inverness-shire, PH25 3EA
Tel: 047982 688
Manchester Host, 30 Naples Street, Manchester M4 4DB. Tel: 061 839 4212
GreenNet; Poptel/GeoNet; both at 25 Downham Rd, London N1 5AA
Tel: 071 249 2948

At the furthest end of the spectrum from the humble amateur bulletin boards are the business on-line conferences, such as those which the Henley Management College ran experimentally for a time in 1989-1990. The idea was that conference participants took part by going on-line as and when other commitments allowed, reading presentations from guest conference 'speakers' and making their own contributions to the subsequent discussion. 'Instead of the usual one or two days full attendance at a conference debate those involved were able to participate over a five week period – dipping in or out of discussion as time allowed,' explained the Henley Management

College, who charged £250 plus VAT for 'attendance' at these on-line conferences. (The college is currently restricting its use of on-line communication to its own staff and students, however.)

CompuServe

CompuServe is a sprawling on-line service of immense proportions, based in Columbus, Ohio. In north America CompuServe has already attracted some 750,000 subscribers, and CompuServe has recently linked up with a Swiss company in a concerted attempt to promote the service in Europe.

CompuServe combines under one umbrella a wide range of on-line facilities. These include an e-mail service, teleshopping (the 'electronic mall'), chat lines and on-line adventure games. Business users have access to on-line database searching. Of more relevance to British users perhaps are the 175 or so on-line conferences which run on CompuServe.

These conferences (known on CompuServe as 'forums') are generally co-ordinated independently of CompuServe by forum system operators ('sysops'). There are a wide range of forums on aspects of computing, many of which solicit contributions from the computer manufacturers and software houses themselves: the forums can therefore be a good way to keep up to date on developments in the industry. There are also forums for professionals – for medics, lawyers and journalists for example – and for like-minded enthusiasts – everything from railway (or, rather, railroad) buffs to goldfish fans.

One forum of particular interest may be the one run for people working from home. The CompuServe directory describes it thus: 'The Working from Home Forum unites those who work from their homes with others who are in similar circumstances. It allows a subscriber to exchange information, make contacts, share resources and solutions to problems, meet other subscribers and keep up-to-date on the latest home/office management tips, resources, laws, tax benefits and marketing approaches.'.

CompuServe has, of course, a strong American feel and bias; European users are still relatively few and far between. Conceivably

CompuServe might provide one way of building up useful US contacts.

INFORMATION

CompuServe, Freepost (BS6971), PO Box 676, Bristol BS99 1NZ.
Tel: 0800 289378

9
THE TECHNICALITIES OF TELEWORKING

Just because you decide to telework shouldn't in general mean that you have to become tangled in a mass of red tape. Nevertheless, there are a number of technical and legal issues which teleworkers, and indeed other home-based workers, need to bear in mind. This chapter looks at some of the more common areas of concern.

Planning issues

Are there any restrictions under planning law on your ability to work from home? It depends: if you were planning to set up in business from home selling, say, scrap metal, the answer would almost certainly be yes – particularly if you were thinking of converting your front garden into the scrap-yard! As a teleworker, however, you are much less likely to have cause for concern.

The question boils down to whether or not you need to apply to your local council, as the planning authority, for planning permission to change the use of part of your house from residential to office usage. According to the planning advisory service, Planning Aid for London, planning permission won't normally be necessary, provided:

- the main use of the house remains as a family home (usually not more than one room should be used for business)
- there are no employees
- there is no nuisance caused to neighbouring properties by deliveries or callers
- there is no external advertising (including a nameplate) on the premises
- there are no trade vehicles parked on the premises

Local authority planning officers are likely to be more concerned if your neighbours start to raise objections to your activities, or if there is noise or disturbance as a result of your work. Fortunately, unlike some other types of home-based activity, teleworking is by and large a quiet sort of occupation: even the noisiest dot-matrix printer is hardly likely to be much of a problem. Neither are you likely to be storing any potentially hazardous or dirty materials for your work on the premises.

On the other hand if your business expands so that you are attracting a regular stream of visitors, or are employing other people in your home, you may need to look into this question more closely. Your local authority planning department will be able to give you more information and advise you whether or not you need planning permission.

Mortgage lenders and landlords

Some home-owners are unsure as to whether they should inform their mortgage lender if they start working from home – and if so, whether the lender will raise objections. It is a sensible precaution to check the provisions of the mortgage agreement you have signed – although in practice the mortgage company's main concern is likely to be simply whether or not you will still be able to meet the monthly mortgage payment.

The Halifax, Britain's largest building society, say that borrowers who begin working from home should get in touch with them, 'if only out of courtesy'. The Halifax's main concern is over insurance (a point we consider below); they add that real problems are only likely to occur if the property ceases to be used primarily for residential purposes – so that in effect the loan has turned into a commercial one.

Tenants who are contemplating teleworking may want to check the clauses of their tenancy agreement. Local authority tenants should have little cause to worry (several local authorities are themselves investigating telework schemes for their own staff).

It is probably equally unlikely that teleworkers who are private tenants will face problems as a result from their landlords. If you find yourself in this situation, seek advice promptly from a housing advisory service or citizens' advice bureau.

Insurance

Insurance may be more of an issue. Teleworkers have probably rather more reason than most to read the small print of their policies, and to check that their work equipment – such as computers and fax machines – are adequately covered.

In many cases, ordinary household contents cover is likely to include at least a certain amount of equipment kept at home but used for work purposes – though insurers sometimes need to be informed of individual items which are of high value. A recent survey by *Which?* magazine found, however, that almost one in three home-based workers who contacted their insurance company were asked to pay a higher premium. If you find that your insurance company will not readily include work equipment in your ordinary contents cover, it may be worth changing to another insurance company who will, rather than insuring your work items separately.

It is also sensible to check the conditions of your building cover. Insurers are naturally concerned if people who are working from home are as a result storing inflammable or hazardous materials or operating dangerous equipment in their houses; teleworkers should be able to reassure insurers on this point.

If you begin to employ other people, remember that you are required by law to take out employer's liability insurance.

If you are teleworking as an employee rather than as self-employed, you should check with your employer that their insurance policies adequately cover equipment kept on your premises. (Their employer's liability insurance may also need to be extended to cover home-based staff.)

Business rates and local taxation

In the pre-Poll Tax days, home-based workers sometimes claimed a part of their rates bill as a business expense (though in doing so they ran the risk of incurring potential Capital Gains Tax liabilities). The Poll Tax (community charge) by contrast is a personal tax on the individual, and cannot be treated as a work expense. The situation may of course change again when the Poll Tax is finally abolished.

In the meantime, there is still the issue of Business Rates to consider. It is possible in some circumstances that a home-based worker may have to pay not only the Poll Tax but also business rates on at least part of the house.

This is a grey area: the Department of the Environment itself admits that 'there will inevitably be difficult cases'. Clearly if you run a shop downstairs and live upstairs you must expect to be liable for business rates on the shop part of your property. But what if you have simply turned a spare room into an office?

The Department of the Environment have issued a Practice Note to local authorities on this point. It is worth quoting from this document:

> 'Property is domestic if it is used *wholly* for the purposes of living accommodation. But "wholly" does not mean "exclusively": and it is therefore considered that some non-domestic use is permitted without rates becoming payable if that use does *not* prevent any of the accommodation from being used for domestic purposes at any time. For example, the use of a home telephone for a mini-cab service or as a call-out number for a plumber would not attract liability for business rates, nor would storage of plumber's tools in the cupboard under the stairs alongside the children's bicycles, even though domestic property is being used as a business "address". Similarly, a person might occasionally work at home, or provide a child-minding service, or a novelist might write books at home, without preventing the property from being used entirely as living accommodation at the same time – by that person or someone else.'

However, the DoE go on to discuss cases where properties have been 'adapted or structurally altered' or where 'equipment or furnishings of a non-domestic nature' have been installed: 'For example, a doctor's or dentist's surgery may occupy one of the rooms in a private house, or a spare room may be converted into an office, with office furniture and equipment... Where, in such circumstances, the local valuation officer is aware of business activity of this sort, it is likely that... the value of the property used for business purposes (but not that used as living accommodation) will be assessed. Liability to pay non-domestic rates will then arise, in addition to any personal community charge payable.'.

As this implies, much will depend in practice on whether the local valuation officer has become aware of the use of the property – or as an article in *The Guardian* put it, 'it is likely that many properties will be overlooked because the owners have assumed themselves exempt and have failed to raise the matter with the authority'.

Taxation and business expenditure

This leads us on to the more general question of how expenditure incurred whilst working at home is taxed. The situation is different depending on whether you are self-employed or an employee.

If you are running your own business, the tax rules state that you can deduct for tax purposes most expenditure incurred 'wholly and exclusively' for the purposes of your business.

You may choose to install separate facilities (such as a second telephone line) for your work use – in which case it will be easy to distinguish between work and private use. But some household bills – gas and electricity bills, for example – may include both work and non-work elements. In circumstances like these, it is normal to apportionate the costs, setting the appropriate work proportion of the total bill against tax. You will need to be able to justify the formula you use to the Inland Revenue. It is frequently advantageous to seek the advice of an accountant in this area.

While domestic users do not have to pay VAT on their fuel and power bills, from July 1990 VAT has been chargeable at the standard rate for business users. This change followed a decision of the European Court, and applies to electricity, gas, oil and solid fuels.

In theory, therefore, home-based workers could face a VAT charge, if they apportion part of their home heating and lighting costs as a business expense. In practice, however, most people working at home will find that their business usage of gas and electricity falls below the VAT threshold: no VAT is payable unless at least 40% of the total fuel bill is for business use. (Furthermore, even if your work use is above the 40% barrier, your total usage of gas and electricity may still exempt you from any VAT liability, if you fall below the minimum levels on which the tax is charged.)

Traditionally, accountants have advised against claiming that any part of your house is used exclusively for work purposes. Capital Gains Tax is not chargeable on a property which is your only or your main home; however, CGT could become liable when you come to sell your house if a part of the property has been used solely for work. In other words, if one-fifth of the property has been treated as work space and your house has increased in value from £20,000 to £120,000, you could face a potential CGT liability on one fifth of the £100,000 increase in value.

In practice, CGT may not be quite such a problem. The indexation allowances mean that increases caused simply by inflation are not taxable; furthermore each taxpayer is entitled to an annual tax-free CGT allowance (currently £5,000). Arguably, too, house prices have settled down after the very rapid price increases in the late 1980s, and in some areas have actually fallen in real terms.

As a result, some accountants are now suggesting that home-based workers may want to reconsider the situation and – always providing that their use of the house justifies it – begin to claim a percentage of their total mortgage interest payments as work expenditure. Before proceeding, it would be sensible to get further advice – and to bear in mind the possible implications of becoming liable for business rates.

If you are teleworking as an employee rather than self-cmployed, your tax situation will be very different. Only expenses which have been incurred by you 'wholly, exclusively and necessarily' in undertaking your employment duties can be set against tax – the extra word 'necessarily' means that in general you will be able to set fewer expenses against tax than if you were self-employed.

If your employer pays some of your household costs these may be treated by the Inland Revenue as taxable perks, subject to extra income tax. Once again, professional advice is sensible.

Self-employed or employed?

Because of the different tax treatment of employees and the self-employed, the Inland Revenue take a considerable interest in this area.

The distinction, in theory, is clear: self-employed people are running their own business, and are free to rise (or fall) by their own efforts. Employees have a contract of employment with their employer, the benefits of agreed employment conditions and the protection which the law offers to workers. However, in practice the dividing line can be less clear-cut, and as we saw in chapter 3 the Inland Revenue may in some cases try to reclassify an apparently self-employed person as an employee.

The Inland Revenue's powers are obviously necessary to prevent companies evading the normal PAYE procedures by artificially claiming that its staff are all self-employed. However some people who feel that they are genuinely self-employed have found that their status has been called into question. Difficulties are particularly likely to occur if almost all your work is done for one client.

The Inland Revenue have produced a leaflet which attempts to clarify the issues. The Revenue say that if you can answer yes to the following questions, you will *usually* be self-employed (their italics!):

- Do you have the final say in how the business is run?
- Do you risk your own money in the business?
- Are you responsible for meeting the losses as well as taking the profits?
- Do you provide the major items of equipment you need to do your job?
- Are you free to hire other people on terms of your own choice to do the work you have taken on? Do you pay them out of your own pocket?
- Do you have to correct unsatisfactory work in your own time and at your own expense?

By contrast, if you answer yes to these questions, you will usually be categorised as an employee:

- Do you yourself have to do the work rather than hire someone else to do it for you?
- Can someone tell you at any time what to do or when and how to do it?
- Are you paid by the hour, week, or month? (Though even if you are paid by commission or on a piecework basis you may still be an employee)
- Do you work set hours, or a given number of hours?
- Do you work at the premises of the person you are working for, or at a place or places they decide?

However, as the Inland Revenue make clear, their notes are 'for guidance only'. The situation is still further complicated because another government department, the Department of Social Security, is also involved. The DSS oversees the National Insurance system; employees (and their employers) pay Class 1 N.I. contributions through the Pay As You Earn system, while the self-employed pay a regular weekly or monthly Class 2 contribution, and are also liable for additional Class 4 contributions on their trading profits. The situation could arise – and indeed has arisen – where an individual is being treated as self-employed by the National Insurance system but as an employee by the Revenue.

If this is an issue which affects you directly, it is sensible to seek professional advice.

INFORMATION

Employed or Self-Employed? A guide for tax and National Insurance, ref IR56/NI39. Available free from Inland Revenue offices

Health and Safety at Work Act

The Health and Safety at Work Act applies to all people at work, whether employees or not. Legally, therefore, teleworkers who are working from home on their own – even if they are self-employed – are covered by the Act, and obliged to abide by its regulations and provisions.

In reality, of course, teleworkers are extremely unlikely to find a Health and Safety Inspector knocking at the door demanding admittance. Nevertheless, there are a number of health and safety issues, particularly around the use of computer equipment, which teleworkers should be aware of. We shall return to this issue in the next chapter.

A recent directive from the European Commission, covering aspects of the design and use of computer monitors ('display screen equipment'), imposes new obligations on employers and workers. It is to be binding on EC member companies from the start of 1993, and will be incorporated into British health and safety legislation.

The Health and Safety Commission have produced a number of free leaflets on aspects of the Health and Safety at Work Act:

- *The Act Outlined* (ref HSC2)
- *Advice to Employers* (ref HSC3)
- *Advice to the Self-employed* (ref HSC4)

These are available from local advice centres, or from the public enquiry offices of the Health and Safety Executive at the addresses below:

INFORMATION

Health and Safety Executive. Public enquiries to: Broad Lane, Sheffield S3 7HQ Tel: 0742 752539; or Baynards House, 1 Chepstow Place, Westbourne Grove, London W2 4TF. Tel: 071 221-0870

Data Protection Act

Finally, it is necessary to point out that teleworkers may need to register under the Data Protection Act. This Act was introduced in 1985 with the commendable intention of protecting the public from the misuse of personal information held on computers.

The Act is very complex, with 43 sections and four schedules, and with a number of exemptions from registration. However, if you keep information about living people on computer for work purposes, the likelihood is that you will have to register. It is an offence not to have registered if you are indeed covered by the provisions of the Act.

The registration fee is currently £75. More information can be obtained from the Office of the Data Protection Registrar, including the useful free pack, *The Data Protection Act: The simpler way for small businesses to register.*

INFORMATION

Data Protection Registrar, Springfield House, Water Lane, Wilmslow, Cheshire SK9 5AX.
Enquiries Tel: 0625 535777

10
HELP WHEN IT'S NEEDED

This final chapter looks at a number of organisations who may be able to help you telework more effectively – and more happily.

OwnBase

What home-based workers need, perhaps, as a way of combatting isolation and possible loneliness is the opportunity to exchange news and to share problems with other people who are also working in the same way.

This, at least, is the reasoning behind OwnBase, an informal grassroots organisation which currently has about 500 members around the country. OwnBase was established in 1986 by a former social worker, Chris Oliver, who found herself engaging in freelance work from home after she and her husband had moved from south Wales to Dorset. 'I had ground to a halt on a long-term solitary self-motivated (and funded) project,' she recalls. 'I was starved for the nourishment of like-minded company.'

Her reaction was to produce a brief newsletter, which she circulated to about a hundred other home-based workers. From that start the OwnBase group has emerged and developed. The organisation describes itself as a 'newsletter network', and the bi-monthly newsletter is still the focus of its activities, although local groups of OwnBase members meet in several parts of the country.

OwnBase say that their group is for 'people whose work, whether for others or for themselves, part- or full-time, paid or unpaid, is done at home'. It is clearly therefore much broader than simply a grouping of teleworkers – indeed, the group say that the occupations engaged in by their members range from A Level marking to aromatherapy, computer consultancy to cake making and inventing to inn sign painting. Nevertheless, the OwnBase newsletter now includes a regular 'teleworking page', contributed by ACRE's Teleworking advisor (see below).

OwnBase are also hoping to encourage greater inter-trading between members, and a new initiative for 1991 has been the publication of a directory of members and their professional skills.

Membership is currently £17.50 a year. More information from the address below (send SAE for free specimen copy of the newsletter):

INFORMATION

OwnBase, c/o 57 Glebe Rd, Egham, Surrey TW20 8BU

Telecommuting Powerhouse

The Telecommuting Powerhouse is an American-style networking and support group, dedicated to encouraging the development of teleworking. The organisation (legally a limited company, although not run on commercial grounds) was established by a professional journalist, Claudia Cragg, who has herself had considerable experience of using on-line services and is an enthusiastic advocate of the telework idea. She stresses the international dimension to teleworking.

The Powerhouse has assembled a skills register of actual and potential teleworkers, and produces a newsletter. Telecommuting Powerhouse members also run telephone advice 'surgeries'. Entries on the skills register are free of charge; an annual subscription of £12 is payable for the newsletter.

INFORMATION

Telecommuting Powerhouse, 27 Old Gloucester St, London WC1.
Tel: 0836 238812 or 071 404 5011
e-mail boxes on several systems, including CompuServe: 71240,2247.

ACRE

As already mentioned, ACRE (the Association of Rural Community Councils in England) has set up a project to help develop interest in telework in country areas of England. Alan Denbigh, their Teleworking Advisor, produces a regular briefing paper on new telework initiatives (available on request), and is also happy to act as a referral point for telephone enquiries. He is also actively involved in proposals to create 'telecottages' in Britain (see below).

ACRE have a number of publications available on issues relating to teleworking.

INFORMATION

ACRE, Somerford Court, Somerford Road, Cirencester GL7 1TW.
Tel: 045 383 4874

Live Wire

A new quarterly magazine for teleworkers, *Live Wire*, was produced for the first time in Spring 1991, from Regent Publishing Ltd.

INFORMATION

Live Wire, Regent Publishing Ltd, 35-37 Brent Street, London NW4 2EF.

Health and safety advice

As already mentioned in the last chapter, teleworkers should be aware of the possible health and safety implications of their work, especially in relation to the use of computer equipment.

There has been considerable publicity recently concerning the dangers of contracting 'repetitive strain injuries' (RSI) from regular use of computer keyboards. These injuries (also sometimes called Upper Limb Disorders or Occupational Overuse Injuries, or named after the tissues involved, such as tenosynovitis) can involve no more than occasional pains and numbness caused from inflammation of tendons and muscles; however, problems can develop to a stage where continued use of a keyboard – and, indeed, continued work – becomes impossible. In one recent well-publicised case, a large number of the Financial Times's journalists were affected, with about 60 employees being forced to take time off-work as a result. The

National Union of Journalists (NUJ) has begun a series of legal actions for damages for members who, the union says, have lost their livelihoods in this way.

RSI, as its name suggests, has been linked to work practices which require rapid repetitive movements of the arm – such as for example the regular use of a set of keys on a computer keyboard. The Health and Safety Executive, the governmental body responsible for workplace health and safety issues, prefers the term Upper Limb Disorders to RSI, and says that other factors are also involved, including 'the need to exert undesirable force, the use of uncomfortable hand grips and the adoption of fixed postures'. However the HSE admits that 'it is time for a real effort to get at the problem and reduce it'.

Badly designed computer equipment and the use of office furniture which encourages poor posture are particular problems: unfortunately they are problems which may be all too likely to be experienced by teleworkers. If you are responsible for buying your own work equipment, the temptation can be to choose cheaper computer equipment with poor quality keyboards and monitors, and to make do with existing chairs and tables. But trying to work at a computer perched on the edge of a rickety table which is too high or low for comfort may be a recipe for longer-term problems.

The HSE has produced guidelines for the correct siting of computer equipment (details are in the booklet *Visual Display Units*, published by HMSO, price £5). Among other things, the HSE suggests that:

- the underside of the worksurface or desk should be high enough to allow adequate thigh clearance; the top of the worksurface should be low enough for the 'home row' of the keyboard to be at elbow height
- the screen should be between 35cms and 60cms away
- the keyboard should be positioned so that your arms are roughly parallel to the floor when typing; the angle at the elbow should be c 70-90 degrees

- the centre of the screen should be placed so that you are looking down at an angle of about 15-20 degrees to see it
- the chair should have an adjustable backrest, and adjustable height

The NUJ point out that traditional desks designed for writing purposes are likely to be too high; the top should ideally be about 70cms off the floor, they say. ('Two inches can make a huge difference.')

There is now a self-help nationwide organisation, the RSI Association, for those people who are suffering from or concerned about RSI. The RSI Association have an information pack available (£1.50 plus large SAE with a 41p stamp). There are also local RSI groups in several parts of the country.

INFORMATION

The RSI Association c/o Christ Church, Redford Way, Uxbridge, Middx UB8 1SZ.

Two other advisory organisations have also published booklets on RSI, and are able to offer further assistance and information:

INFORMATION

City Centre, 32-35 Featherstone St, London EC1Y 8QX Tel: 071 608 1338
London Hazards Centre, 3rd Floor, Headland House, 308 Gray's Inn Road, London WC1X 8DS. Tel: 071 837 5605

Both these organisations have helpful information available on other health and safety issues relating to computer usage. City Centre, for example, have published a *VDU Hazards Factpack* (price £3), including details on issues such as eye strain and skin complaints. They also continue to stress the possible hazards for pregnant women of working at visual display units (monitors), and say that studies have found an increased risk of miscarriage from women who have worked at computer screens during their pregnancies. The official position of the HSE, however, is that any such link is as yet unproven.

INFORMATION

The Health and Safety Executive has a free leaflet, *Working with VDUs*. Two other more technical publications, *Visual Display Units* (£5) and *Work Related Upper Limb Disorders* (£3.75) are published by HMSO
Health and Safety Executive. Public enquiries to: Broad Lane,
Sheffield S3 7HQ Tel: 0742 752539; or Baynards House, 1 Chepstow Place, Westbourne Grove, London W2 4TF. Tel: 071 221-0870

Telecottages: out from the home

It may seem perverse to conclude a book with the title this one bears on its cover by suggesting that the home need not be the only base for successful teleworking. However it's worth remembering that distance work using computer and telecommunications technology doesn't necessarily mean home-based work. In some circumstances home may indeed not be the most suitable place to locate your work.

It's worth briefly drawing attention therefore to the interest that is currently being shown in the idea of 'telecottages', small community-based centres which can provide sophisticated computer and telecoms facilities on an agency basis to people in the locality.

The telecottage idea comes from Scandinavia; indeed, the first 'community teleservice centre' there opened in Sweden in 1985, in a remote village called Vemdalen, close to the Norwegian border. The aim was to open up the opportunities and benefits of information technology to a very thinly populated area, for use both by local business and by community organisations. There are now about 25 similar telecottages in Sweden, some run as non-profit ventures but most privately owned and orientated towards small local enterprises. Both Norway and Denmark have about ten similar telecottage ventures apiece.

In Britain, the idea of telecottages has been greeted with some enthusiasm by organisations like ACRE and Highlands and Islands Enterprise (formerly Highlands and Islands Development Board) concerned with rural economic development. In a very different environment, Manchester City Council are exploring ways of developing 'electronic village halls', using the facilities of the Manchester

Host (see page 93) on several city estates. A handful of telecottages are now operating and several more are under consideration.

The term 'telecottage' is a powerful one, perhaps misleadingly so. In practice, a traditional agency offering computer or fax facilities to small businesses may be able to offer at least some of the same services. Nevertheless, the interest in telecottages (and related ideas, like the proposal for a 'televillage' in a remote part of Herefordshire) suggests that the teleworking concept still has the power to enthuse people and to stimulate new ideas.

INFORMATION

ACRE, Somerford Court, Somerford Road, Cirencester GL7 1TW.
Tel: 045 383 4874
Highlands and Islands Enterprise, Bridge House, 20 Bridge Street, Inverness IV1 1QR. Tel: 0463 234171

APPENDIX 1   PACKET SWITCHING USING BT'S DIALPLUS SERVICE

This appendix lists the local access points (nodes) to BT's packet switching service Dialplus. For more information see page 000.

Aberdeen	0224	210701
Ayr	0292	611822
Belfast	0232	331284
Benbecula	0870	2657
Birmingham	021	633 3474
Brechin	03562	5782
Brecon	0874	3151
Brighton	0273	550045
Bristol	0272	211545
Cambridge	0223	460127
Campbelltown	0586	52298
Canterbury	0227	762950
Cardiff	0222	344184
Carlisle	0228	512621
Chelmsford	0245	491323
Cheltenham	0242	227547
Crewe	0270	588531
Dalmally	08382	410
Dundee	0382	22452
Dunoon	0369	2210
Edinburgh	031	313 2137
Elgin	0343	543890
Exeter	0392	421565
Glasgow	041	204 1722
Golspie	04083	3021
Grimsby	0472	353550
Guildford	0483	38632
Halifax	0422	349224
Hastings	0424	722788

Huntly	0466	3653
Invergarry	08093	406
Inverness	0463	711940
Ipswich	0473	210212
Kings Lynn	0553	691090
Kingussie	0540	661078
Kinross	0577	63111
Kirkwall	0856	6004
Leamington Spa	0926	451419
Leeds	0532	440024
Leicester	0533	628092
Lerwick	0595	6211
Lincoln	0522	532398
Liverpool	051	255 0230
Llandrindod Wells	0597	825881
Llandudno	0492	860500
Lochcarron	05202	598
Lochgilphead	0546	3717
Lochinver	05714	548
London (Clerkenwell)	071	490 2200
London (Colindale)	081	905 9099
London (Croydon)	081	681 5040
London (Monument)	071	283 9123
Luton	0582	481818
Machynlleth	0654	703560
Mallaig	0687	2728
Manchester	061	834 5533
Melvich	06413	364
Middlesbrough	0642	245464
Mintlaw	0771	24560
Neath	0639	641650
Newcastle	091	261 6858
Northampton	0604	33395
Norwich	0603	763165
Nottingham	0602	506005
Oban	0631	63111

Oxford	0865	798949
Petersfield	0730	65098
Peterborough	0733	555705
Plymouth	0752	603302
Poole	0202	666461
Port Ellen	0496	2143
Portree	0478	3208
Preston	0772	204405
Reading	0734	500722
Rotherham	0709	820402
Rugeley	0889	576610
Sedgwick	0539	561263
Sevenoaks	0732	740966
Shrewsbury	0743	231027
Southampton	0703	634530
Stornoway	0851	6111
Strathdon	09756	51396
Swindon	0793	541620
Taunton	0823	335667
Tobermory	0688	2060
Truro	0872	223864
Warminster	0985	846091
Wick	0955	4537
York	0904	625625
Vodafone gateway		970970

APPENDIX 2 FURTHER READING

Practical details, including information about publications of direct relevance and use to teleworkers, have been included in the appropriate places in the text.

This selected list of books, magazine articles and other published material is designed for two purposes: to help identify sources used in this book and to assist those readers who want to explore more of the literature written on teleworking. It is not intended to be comprehensive (for more detailed bibliographies, try the two publications marked with an asterisk below).

Books and Publications

Communications for Progress, A Guide to International e-mail; Graham Lane   (CIIR, 1990)

A Guide to Working from Home; British Telecom (n.d.)

Homeworking and the New Technology - The Reality and the Rhetoric; Mike Brocklehurst (published in *Personnel Review* vol 18, no 2 1989)

International Data Services User Guide; British Telecom (1989)

IT Futures Surveyed; NEDO (1986)

Networking in Organisations: The Rank Xerox Experiment; P Judkins, D West, J Drew (Gower, 1985)

New Hacker's Handbook; Hugo Cornwall, rev. Steve Gold (Century, 1989)

The New Homeworkers; Ursula Huws (Low Pay Unit, 1984)

On Line Business Sourcebook; Pamela Foster and Allan Foster (Headland Press, 1990)

Telecommunications in Rural England; Rural Development Commission (1989)

The Telecommuters; Francis Kinsman (John Wiley, 1987)

Telecommuting: How to Make it work for You and Your Company; Marcia Kelly and Gil Gordon (Prentice-Hall, 1986)

Telecommuting: The Organisational and Behavioral Effects of Working from Home; Reagan Mays Ramsower (UMI Research Press, 1985)

Telework; Conditions of Work Digest, vol 9, 1/1990 (International Labour Organisation)*

Telework: Impact on Living and Working Conditions; Sylvie Craipeau and Jean-Claude Marot (European Foundation for the Improvement of Living and Working Conditions, 1984)

Telework, Towards the Elusive Office; U Huws, W Korte and S Robinson (John Wiley, 1990)*

Teleworking and Telecottages, ACRE/Centre for Rural Studies, Royal Agricultural College (1990)

The Third Wave; Alvin Toffler (Collins/Pan, 1980)

Tomorrow's Workplace, Harnessing the Challenge of Teleworking; Henley Centre for Forecasting (1988)

Tomorrow's Workplace, The Manager's Guide to Teleworking; Francis Kinsman; British Telecom (n.d.)

Magazine and Journal articles

'Hard Day's Work in the Electronic Office, A'; Kathleen Christensen (*Across the Board*, April 1987)

'Home Teleworking – A Study of its Pioneers'; Joanne Pratt (*Technological Forecasting and Social Change*, vol 25, 1984)

'Home Truths About Teleworking', John and Celia Stanworth (*Personnel Management*, Nov 1989)

'Homeworking through New Technology – Opportunities and Opposition'; Sean Connolly (*Industrial Management and Data Systems*, Sep/Oct 1988 and Nov/Dec 1988)

'Impacts of Computer-Mediated Home-Based Work on Women and Their Families'; Kathleen Christensen (*Office: Technology and People*, Nov 1987)

'Myth of the Electronic Cottage, The'; Tom Forester (*Futures*, June 1988)

'Promoting Work/Family Balance'; Douglas Hall (*Organisational Dynamics*, Winter 1990)

'Social Construction of Technology, The: Microcomputers and the Organisation of Work'; Barbara Risman and Donald Tomaskovic-Devey (*Business Horizons*, May-June 1989)

'Teleworking - Splendid Isolation?' (*Labour Research*, February 1991)

'Uprooting the Office'; Ursula Huws and others (*Practical Computing*, Sep 1989)

'Waiting for the Telecommuter'; Geoff Tyler (*Management Accounting*, March 1989)

INDEX

ABI/Inform 69, 74
Abroad, teleworking 6, 12, 18
ACRE 28, 107–8, 111–12
Answering phones 47–8, 52
Banking, home 53, 84–5
British Telecom 6, 11, 12, 27–30, 39, 40–2, 45–51, 62–5, 69–71, 80–6, 88–9
Bulletin boards 59, 91, 94–5
Business rates 98–100, 101
Cable TV 42
Capital Gains Tax 98, 101
Children and telework 13, 21, 30–2
CIX 92
Community Charge – see Poll Tax
Company information, on-line 73
CompuServe 94–5
Computer communications 54–66
Computers and telework 52, 54–7, 103–4, 108–10
Confederation of British Industry (CBI) 6, 11, 12
Country, teleworking in the 26–30, 37, 45, 107–8, 111–12
Data bits 59
Data Protection Act 104–5
Data-Star 69, 74–6
DIALOG 69, 74–6
Dialplus 62–5, 70, 113–15
Digital telephone exchanges 44, 48–9, 58
Disabilities and telework 21
Electronic cottage 13
Electronic mail 52–3, 59, 63, 77, 85, 87–91, 94–5
Electronic Yellow Pages 68, 70–1, 84
E-mail – see Electronic mail

Employers attitudes to telework 11–15, 16–17, 22–3
Employment conditions and telework 13–14, 34–36
Equal Opportunities Commission 14, 34, 35, 38
ESA-IRS 76
European Community, on-line services 78
Fax transmission 41, 51–3, 90–1
FI Group 12, 17, 22
Gaelic language 93
GeoNet 77, 89, 93
Government information, on-line services 83–4
Grants available 37
Health and safety 25–6, 103–4, 108–11
Henley Centre for Forecasting 6, 7
Highlands and Islands Initiative 27
ICL 17
Income tax – see Taxation and telework
Insurance 34, 36, 98
International Labour Office 30
International packet switching 63, 65
ISDN 44, 58
Local authorities and telework 18, 96–7, 98–100
Manchester Host 89, 93, 111–12
Men and telework 23–4, 33
Mercury Communications 29, 40–3, 45–6, 51–3, 63
Micronet 83, 85
Minitel 80, 86
Mobile telephones 29–30, 43–4, 49–51
Modems 55–61
Mortgage lenders and telework 97
National Insurance 36, 103

Nilles, Jack 13, 15
Office, equipping an 26, 109–10
On-line conferences 92–4
On-line databases 58, 61, 63, 67–79
OwnBase 38, 106–7
Packet switching 62–3, 113–15
Parity checking 59–61
Pay levels and telework 14–15, 34
PCNs 43–4, 49
Phone Base 69–70, 84
Planning permission 96–7
Poll Tax 98–9
Prestel 58, 70, 80–6
Profile 69, 71–3
Rank Xerox 16–17, 32, 35
Repetitive strain injuries (RSI) 26, 108–10
Scotland 27, 28, 37, 92–3, 111–12
Self-employment 14–17, 35–37, 100–3
Taxation and telework 36–7, 100–3

Telecom Gold 63–5, 72, 77, 82, 88–91
Telecommuting Powerhouse 107
Telecottages 108, 111–12
Telephone services 40–53
Telepoint 51
Teleshopping 84–5, 94
Télétel 80, 86
Teletext – see Videotex
Telex 52, 90–1
Toffler, Alvin 12–13, 32
Trade unions 22
UK On-Line User Group 78
VAT 36, 100–1
Videoconferencing 49
Videotex 80–6
Viewdata – see Videotex
Voicemail 47–8
Women and telework 13–14, 23–4, 32–3, 110
Workaholism 25